COVERING
THE COURTS

Media Studies Series

COVERING THE COURTS

Free Press, Fair Trials & Journalistic Performance

ROBERT GILES
ROBERT W. SNYDER Editors

Transaction Publishers
New Brunswick (U.S.A.) and London (U.K.)

Library of Congress Catalog Number: 98-26638
ISBN: 0-7658-0462-X
Printed in the United States of America

Library of Congress Cataloging-in-Publication Data

Covering the courts : free press, fair trials, and journalistic performance / edited by Robert Giles and Robert W. Snyder.
    p. cm. — (Media studies series)
Originally published in the Media studies journal, winter 1998.
Includes bibliographical references and index.
ISBN 0-7658-0462-X (pbk. : alk. paper)
    1. Free press and fair trial—United States. 2. Conduct of court proceedings—United States. 3. Newspaper court reporting—United States. 4. Mass media and criminal justice—United States. I. Giles, Robert H., 1933– . II. Snyder, Robert W., 1955– . III. Series.
KF9223.5.C68   1998
347.73'12—dc21
                                             98-26638
                                              CIP

Contents

"If Canada is to Americans a foreign country, its foreign-ness is to be found in the British character of its political practices, its public institutions and its legal system," writes a Canadian scholar of media law. "[S]ensational cases in Canada are less sensational and less likely to produce the circuses that marked several American trials in recent years—most notably the trial of O.J. Simpson."

Part II: Cameras in the Courts

The chief anchor and managing editor of Court TV wrestles with fundamental questions about cameras in the courts: "Is the sole function of the courts to dispense justice between competing parties, so that any proposed measures to inform the public should be rejected if they might conceivably affect a trial? Or is opening the courts to the public a value in itself, which should be accommodated unless there is some showing that the quality of justice would be diminished?"

A *New Yorker* writer who covered the trials of O.J. Simpson and Timothy McVeigh concludes: "Every reasonable person concedes that the Oklahoma City bombing, with its toll of 168 dead, was a more important event. But it was the Simpson case that evoked the passionate and enduring reaction."

"When there's a camera in the courtroom in a criminal case, generally people are on their better behavior," recalls a lawyer from the Simpson criminal trial defense team. "You make it a fair trial. You get everybody thinking in higher terms."

"Never in my 30 years of covering trials have I entered a courtroom with the objective of creating entertainment," writes a special correspondent for the Associated Press. "Social history, yes; entertainment, no."

Andrew Tyndall

A 10-year survey by a veteran analyst of network news broadcasts finds: "Only the Persian Gulf War received more minutes of airtime on the nightly news than the O.J. Simpson trial."

Tony Mauro

"It is an accepted if mysterious anomaly that the federal courts, and especially the Supreme Court, march to their own music when it comes to cameras in the courts," writes a veteran Supreme Court reporter. "What is routinely accepted in most state courts is still unheard of, and largely dreaded, in federal courthouses."

Katherine Krupp

"A skillful courtroom sketch has some advantages over a photograph," notes an art historian who curated an exhibit on courtroom artists. "It absorbs physical and emotional elements beyond the reach of the stationary courtroom video lens, with its monocular perspective that flattens depth and ignores dramatic detail."

Part III: Cross-Examinations

Judge Judith S. Kaye

"Our democracy depends on a strong court system, and a strong court system in turn depends on public support and confidence," argues the chief judge of the state of New York. "And if the only cases covered are a few depicted as mindlessly releasing dangerous criminals, how much respect can citizens have for the courts?"

Interview with Judge Richard S. Arnold
and Judge Gilbert S. Merritt

Two federal appellate judges who have helped to set national judicial policy explore the relationship between the news media and the administration of justice. "Judges need to understand better that we operate only by the consent of the governed," observes one. "And the press is a major part of the consent of the governed."

A New York City sex crimes prosecutor surveys the media and concludes, "The overwhelming coverage that the public sees is tabloid coverage, which still tends to sensationalize and emphasize the tawdrier side of the cases."

"We see now, in high-profile cases, a ravenous appetite on the part of the press to obtain information that they have no legal right to get," observes an attorney who has defended both the indigent and O.J. Simpson. "And when they get it and disclose it, it undermines the fairness of our trial processes."

The former prosecutor for the International War Crimes Tribunals for the former Yugoslavia and Rwanda proposes the creation of a "Genocide Watch": "The involvement, if not the leadership, of journalists would be essential."

Part IV: Review Essay

Surveying books about the Supreme Court that range from deferential to skeptical, a Harvard law professor who once clerked for Supreme Court Justice Thurgood Marshall concludes that "journalists should inform the public fully about the Court, even if doing so will likely undermine public respect for the justices. They should not act as the justices' publicists."

Preface

The fascination of the press and the public with the high-profile criminal trials of O.J. Simpson and Timothy McVeigh forms the backdrop for our extensive examination of court coverage. Three themes are evident:

First, journalists have expanded their role beyond chronicling the testimony and observing the action in the courtroom. They are intensely involved in reporting every step of the process, from arrest through verdict. It is the reporters who are the interlocutors between the judicial system and the public. For better or worse, news accounts are how the vast majority of citizens experience trials.

Second, parties to a trial work hard at playing to the press. The police, seeking credit for a criminal investigation, parade suspects before the television cameras, knowing that the public is willing to accept an arrest as confirmation of guilt. Defense attorneys use the courthouse steps for theater, playing to crowds of reporters and photographers in their quest for sympathetic portrayals of their clients. Prosecutors query reporters on whether a line of attack in a case seems plausible. Occasionally, judges talk off the record to reporters to reinforce the subtle points of their decisions.

Third, there is a strong case for cameras in the courts, especially in the federal appellate courts and the U.S. Supreme Court. In an age when the press is the citizens' gateway to the world in which they live, cameras are an effective way of guaranteeing that trials are truly public and open to everyone. The real obstacle to wider use of cameras in the courts is not the concept of openness, but rather the tendency of television news to squeeze the taped images from the courtroom into sound bites.

Linda Deutsch, who has covered the courts for 30 years for the Associated Press, tells of her struggle in an age of television "to cling to objectivity in spite of the seemingly endless public thirst for opinions in the case." Drawing on lessons learned from others, she offers a context for court reporting as wise as it is fundamental: Report what happens in the courtroom. Resist attempts to be drawn into the leaking and spinning game by either the defense or the prosecution. "A lawyer pontificating on the courthouse steps may provide a good sound bite, but an expert witness calmly explaining the pattern of knife wounds or the trajectory of bullets will have a greater impact on the trial's outcome."

In an interview, Barry Scheck, a law professor and veteran defense attorney, says the "perennial tension" at the heart of free press/fair trial controversies is intensified by the desire of the press "to know privileged information that should not be disclosed if you are going to have a fair trial.... When you disclose this kind of information prior to the trial, and the information comes out in a fashion that is not orderly and not within the trial process itself, you will skew the process and make it unfair."

No better example exists, he says, than the publication by the *Dallas Morning News* of conversations between Timothy McVeigh and his lawyers.

Judge Gilbert S. Merritt of the U.S. Court of Appeals for the 6th Circuit and a leading proponent of cameras in trial coverage, says in an interview that the prospects for cameras in federal courts will ultimately turn on how cameras are used in the lower courts.

He urges the press to set standards for court coverage that would address, among other things, the tendency of television news to show the story of a trial in sound bites.

Reporters' conduct and the news they produce should present an intelligence and dignity of purpose that make a case for further use of cameras. What if producers asked themselves before they air a story: If the sentiment for and against cameras in federal courts was equally balanced, how would this piece change this balance?

If cameras showing trials are a good thing, as several of our contributors believe, one way to overcome the sound-bite problem is to create a C-SPAN for the courts with programming that would enable audiences to follow trials from opening statements to verdict.

Fred Graham of Court TV makes the point that the virtue of public trials with cameras is not endorsed by judges for three reasons: One is the fear of appearing inept on camera. Second is the mindset that it is unseemly for judges to appear on camera. Third, "Some judges appear to place no value on the opportunity for the public to see justice in progress—so that any countervailing factor, however questionable and speculative, tips the scales toward banning TV coverage."

Judith S. Kaye, chief judge of the state of New York, writes that giving the courts the attention they deserve as a branch of government means looking at them between big trials and big verdicts. She can't talk about her decisions. But she can speak about the courts between decisions. And her branch of government does much that falls outside conventional trial coverage.

"Sitting judges can't hold press conferences about their decisions. They must remain above the fray, preserve their impartiality and let their decisions speak for themselves. That best serves the law and all society. A decision should stand as the last word. But this means that when judges are sound bitten, they can't bite back. And since our writings are rarely reproduced in the popular press, the critical spin goes unanswered and unjust labels stick."

Judge Kaye issues an invitation: "It's time we began speaking—or, more significantly, listening—to one another. Too many important interests are at stake to do otherwise."

We agree. The press, the bench and the bar each have a stake in a free press, in fair trials and in strong, independent courts. We hope this issue of *Media Studies Journal* will encourage the conversation.

Our regular readers will recognize changes in the size and look of the *Journal*. Dale Peskin, assistant managing editor for development of the *Dallas Morning News* and a leader in innovative newspaper design, worked with our editors and Tom Whitridge of Ink, Inc. to create a design that blends the classic with the contemporary. It begins with a larger format that is easier to read. The typeface is Garamond, which dates to the 16th century. "It is," says Peskin, "sturdy and elegant"— like the arguments of our writers.

—The Editors

I

Free Press, Fair Trial

"Brennan, the most influential intellectual force of the Court during the last half of the 20th century, believed the presence of the press in the courthouse gallery did not diminish the Sixth Amendment rights of the accused.... For him, fair trials existed because of free press."

—Bruce Sanford

1

No Contest

Bruce W. Sanford

When the phrases "free press" and "fair trial" roll off the tongue, the word *versus* is usually sandwiched between them.

The two Anglo-American ideals are presented as if they were inherently at odds with each other, as if they were mutually exclusive. Rarely are we offered the possibility of enjoying both.

But this is one trumped-up "conflict" that we can't blame on television. As Chief Justice Warren Burger wrote more than 20 years ago, the problems created by the collision between the First and the Sixth amendments are "almost as old as the Republic." Aaron Burr's 1807 prosecution for treason, he noted, provoked so much courtroom drama, and accompanying publicity, that commentators fretted about whether incendiary newspaper coverage would incinerate the possibility for a fair trial. Chief Justice John Marshall rejected Burr's argument.

The evolution of a body of law to govern these clashes took more than a century and a half to unfold, however. And when the Supreme Court finally started to face the tough questions surrounding press freedom and the right to a fair trial in the 1960s and '70s, it was in the midst of aggressively expanding the boundaries of both: Journalists *and* criminal defendants have been among the great winners in modern constitutional law. Indeed, if one overarching theme is discernible from the High Court's pronouncements of the past 40 years, it is, quite simply, that judges need a vigorous, probing, enterprising media to ensure both a criminal defendant's rights and public confidence in our system of justice.

Since the mid-1980s, however, the Court's voice has gone quiet. For more than a decade, not one decision has addressed the media's First Amendment rights to cover the courts. The silence undoubtedly reflects a judicial attitude toward the ubiquitous media that, like the rest of the country's, borders on contempt. The silence suggests that future activity in this corner of the law will likely occur at the margins rather than through bold new pronouncements. And in recent years the privacy interests of jurors and witnesses have become a paramount consideration in the courtroom, adding a new dimension to judges' efforts to balance the rights of the media and the rights of the accused.

When the free press/fair trial issue arrived at the Supreme Court in the 1960s, it was clothed as a Sixth Amendment matter rather than a First Amendment one. In that decade, the justices, well launched on their odyssey to revolutionize criminal procedure, struck down a number of convictions based on unfair publicity.

In *Estes v. Texas,* decided in 1965, the Court reviewed the prosecution of Billy Sol Estes, a buccaneer financier, for fraud. Both a pretrial hearing, as well as parts of the trial itself, were broadcast on television. The pretrial hearing in particular was marked by massive disruption from camera crews—an ironic footnote given that it was called to decide whether to permit television coverage during the trial.

The Court said that Estes was so thoroughly harmed by these events that it would depart from its normal rule and reverse his conviction without looking for particular ways in which he was actually prejudiced. (The opinion amounted to an early indictment of televised trials that left a constitutional odor for more than 15 years, until the Court in 1981 said that broadcasting trials does not intrinsically violate the Sixth Amendment.) But while criticizing television's impact on the trial, the Court in *Estes* did not say much about how to control coverage without obliterating it. The First Amendment side of the equation, in other words, was not brought into play.

The Court began to pay more serious attention to the free press/fair trial issue a year later when it was confronted with the egregious excesses of the Sam Sheppard murder trial. Here was a courtroom "circus" out of control. Trial judge Edward Blythin, a former mayor of Cleveland, gave daily interviews, reporters roamed the courtroom like proprietary floorwalkers and the Supreme Court—normally restrained in its descriptions—conjured up Fellini images by labeling it a "Roman holiday." To hardly anyone's surprise, except, perhaps, *Cleveland Press* editor Louis Seltzer, who hounded the philandering physician with avenging coverage, Dr. Sam's conviction for the gory slaying of his pregnant wife was reversed. "Let's get a grip," the High Court seemed to say. "And, for God's sake (or justice's), let's have some decorum.

Let's keep these, ahem, journalists in their place before they spoil everything."

In overturning Sheppard's conviction, the justices went a bit further than they had in *Estes*—this time, they laid out some suggestions to trial judges for managing press coverage.

For starters, the Court endorsed limiting the number of reporters in the courtroom. It also proposed insulating witnesses from the media and issuing gag orders to prevent lawyers from granting out-of-court interviews. Additionally, the Court said that news organizations could be warned about publishing information not introduced into evidence. Other strategies put forward were to sequester juries, transfer cases to far-away venues and postpone trials.

All of these measures were advanced by a Court that just two years earlier, in the landmark libel case of *New York Times v. Sullivan,* had committed the nation to developing a speech marketplace that would be "uninhibited, robust, and wide-open." That marketplace, it became clear, would have to look different when criminal defendants, as opposed to libel plaintiffs, were in the picture.

In the wake of *Sheppard,* reporters found themselves increasingly hobbled in their court coverage by gag orders issued against the press itself. These prior restraints were virtually wiped out by *Nebraska Press* in a majority opinion written, ironically, by Anglophile Warren Burger, which said we would be different from England—we would not muzzle court coverage. In that case, lower courts in Nebraska had directed news organizations not to disseminate accounts of confessions made by an accused murderer, nor to publish other facts that were "strongly implicative" of his guilt. This time, when the free press/fair trial issue arrived at the Supreme Court, it was dressed in First Amendment clothes because the gag order had been challenged by several state press and broadcast associations.

The Court said for the first time that such gag orders were presumptively unconstitutional. Chief Justice Burger analyzed the issue within the long line of precedent frowning on prior restraints, which he called the "most serious" and "least tolerable" of infringements on speech rights. For a Court that had given a green light to the *New York Times* and the *Washington Post* five years earlier to print the Pentagon Papers despite the cries of harm to national security, it did not seem a great leap to allow the publication of material relating to a murder trial in Nebraska.

While the Court in *Sheppard* had listed strategies for combating unfair publicity with little regard for how those measures might affect the functioning of the media, in *Nebraska Press* it went over the same ground with an eye for using techniques that would not directly interfere with what journalists could write or broadcast, such as the careful screening of jurors during the voir dire process. From 1966 to 1976, the Court's emphasis had shifted seismically.

If the clear message of *Nebraska Press* was that the media must be free to publish what it can find out, it did not prevent judges from hindering coverage of trials through indirect means—by choking off sources of information. The Supreme Court indicated that the standards for limiting what attorneys can say to the press are less exacting than for limiting what the press can say to the public. Consequently, the placing of gag orders on lawyers continues to be a common practice in high-stakes criminal proceedings.

Another indirect means to curtail publication of bothersome information is simply to close the courthouse door to the press and public. In 1979, the Supreme Court seemed to approve of just such a tactic in *Gannett v. DePasquale.* In *Gannett,* two persons on trial for murder requested the closure of a pretrial suppression hearing. The prosecution did not oppose the defendants' motion, and the trial judge agreed.

When the Court reviewed the judge's decision, the question was presented as a Sixth Amendment one—to whom does the constitutional guarantee of a "public trial" belong? The answer, according to the Court, was that it belongs to the defendant—and neither the public nor the press can use the Sixth Amendment to compel open proceedings if the accused does not want it. The Court completely ducked the First Amendment side of the issue, saying only that the trial judge had given "all appropriate deference" to these considerations before closing the suppression hearing.

"All appropriate deference?" That sounds like a First Amendment executioner's song. Justice William Rehnquist, in a concurring opinion, sang the last verse. He wrote that once the parties agree to exclude the public from a trial, the judge does not have to make any further inquiry. And he also took up the free speech implications that the Court itself avoided and made a severe conclusion: The public and the press do not have any right to attend judicial proceedings under the First Amendment.

Gannett closed the decade of the 1970s on a depressing, one-sided and perhaps even predictable note. Earlier in the 1970s, news organizations had argued that "the public's right to know" could be leveraged to secure journalists special privileges to visit prisons and obtain government-controlled information. The press had also asked to be exempt from obligations that compromised its news-gathering capabilities, such as testifying at grand jury hearings about confidential sources. The Supreme Court, however, roundly rejected any version of the "right to know" each time the media brought it forward.

But something about *Gannett,* and its implications for the public, as well as the press, rattled a common nerve. As detailed by Lucas Powe Jr. in *The Fourth Estate and the Constitution,* angry criticism and protests erupted after America's newspaper publishers erected a huge cardboard, seven-layer cake dedicated to the imperiled First Amendment in the lobby of the Waldorf-Astoria Hotel. The sagging monster looked as if it might march on Washington. Meeting in New York, several justices, in unusual public comments, hastily retreated from the case— including Chief Justice Burger, who said that the opinion's holding only applied to pretrial proceedings and had been misread by lower courts. In the year after *Gannett* was decided, 272 motions were filed nationwide to close criminal proceedings, according to Powe, and 33 trials were closed outright. Clearly, the Court had goofed, overemphasizing Sixth Amendment interests and overlooking the First Amendment values that contribute to a fair trial.

It didn't take long for the Court to reverse course, and when it did, it created a brand new First Amendment right out of whole cloth.

A year later, in *Richmond Newspapers v. Virginia,* a state judge had closed the murder trial of John Paul Stevenson with a simple one-sentence order, citing *Gannett.* In a previous stage of the case, the judge had declared a mistrial when a prospective juror had apparently informed others of a news article reporting that Stevenson's earlier conviction for the crime had been thrown out on appeal.

When the Supreme Court took up the case, the First Amendment access question this time was squarely before it. And while the Court by no means spoke with a single voice (there were six opinions for the seven justices in the majority), it delivered a remarkably important message: Trials such as Stevenson's are presumed to be open to the press and public, although the words of the Constitution nowhere commanded it. Not since *New York Times v. Sullivan* had the Court taken such a breathtaking constitutional step in the free speech area.

Chief Justice Burger justified the Court's action as a matter of tradition, finding strong support in his beloved Anglo-American jurisprudence for open trials. To this historical consideration, Justice William Brennan Jr.'s concurring opinion added another doctrinal point: Access should be favored when it contributes to the functioning of the judicial process in question.

Brennan's theoretical framework has been the driving force behind the extension of *Richmond Newspapers'* presumption of openness to other aspects of the criminal justice system. There have been only three other High Court decisions developing this new First Amendment right of access of the public (and its "surrogate," the press) to attend criminal proceedings. All followed quickly on the heels of *Richmond Newspapers.*

In 1982, in *Globe Newspaper v. Superior Court,* the Court struck down a Massachusetts statute that required judges to exclude the public from proceedings at which juvenile victims of sex offenses were scheduled to testify. State statutes needed to confer discretion and flexibility on judges, not automatic orders. Two years later in California, in *Press-Enterprise v. Riverside County,* the Court held that only on rare occasions could judges conduct voir dire behind closed doors, such as when intense privacy interests of potential jurors are at stake. And in 1986, in another case involving the *Press-Enterprise,* the Court said that since preliminary hearings function essentially in the place of trials, they too are held to a rule of presumptive openness.

No two justices wrote more of the key opinions in the free press/fair trial field than Burger and Brennan. In their decisions, however, one finds strikingly different conceptions of the role of the media. In *Nebraska Press,* Burger looks back at the *Sheppard* case and concludes: "Beyond doubt the press had shown no responsible concern for the constitutional guarantee of a fair trial." Later in that opinion, he observes that the First Amendment places something akin to a fiduciary duty on the press—"a duty widely acknowledged but not always observed by editors and publishers." For Burger, therefore, the equation seems to be "fair trial *despite* free press."

Yet Brennan, the most influential intellectual force of the Court during the last half of the 20th century, believed the presence of the press in the courthouse gallery did not diminish the Sixth Amendment rights of the accused but actually enhanced them. "Public access," he wrote in *Richmond Newspapers,* "acts as an important check, akin in purpose to the other checks and balances that infuse our system of government." And in *Globe Newspaper,* he further explained his structural conception of the First Amendment, arguing that open trials ensure that a "constitutionally-protected discussion of government affairs is an informed one." For him, fair trials existed *because* of free press.

The Supreme Court has ignored the *Richmond Newspapers* thread for more than 10 years now, suggesting that it has gone as far as it intends to go in opening up the judicial system and the wealth of information that is filed in documents and testimony in both criminal and civil cases. No one expects the Court to uncloak the secrecy of grand jury proceedings, for example. Such a move would not be supported by historical tradition, nor would it appear to enhance the functioning of the investigative task that grand juries are called to perform.

In lower courts, nevertheless, the accumulated Supreme Court wisdom of the 1960s, '70s and '80s requires judges to use carefully tailored means whenever they try to exclude the press from the courtroom. Instinct or outrage is not enough—they must find a substantial probability that the defendant's right to a fair hearing is endangered, that closing the proceedings would avert this threat and that no reasonable alternatives to closure exist. Like all multipronged tests in constitutional law, this standard gives judges some flexibility and enables them to meet the day-to-day crises that pop up in criminal trials.

In celebrated cases, some judges can forget these rules. Lance Ito impulsively closed off all the O.J. Simpson jury voir dire despite the irony that it was a similar closure in his own state court system that had triggered the 1984 *Press-Enterprise* case a mere decade earlier. Ito's mistake was righted quickly enough, but it revealed the need (even after clear-cut Supreme Court decisions) for the press to have lawyers ready on short notice to prevent judges from drifting back to a pre-*Richmond Newspapers* mindset.

In contrast to Judge Ito, Richard Matsch, the well-respected judge who presided over the trial of Timothy McVeigh for the Oklahoma City bombing, used carefully calibrated means of controlling press access to certain sources of information and proceedings. To be sure, he heard a din of media objections along the way, but he has been widely credited with pulling off a serious and successful trial.

Matsch issued two gag orders over lawyers involved in the case, the second of which was put in effect during jury selection and was so far-reaching that it prohibited all out-of-court statements. He also showed extraordinary concern for the privacy of the jury, a solicitude first sanctioned in *Press-Enterprise:* The court did not release jurors' names, scrambled the identification numbers by which potential panel members were known during the screening process and conducted so-called for cause challenges to particular jurors outside of public view. Matsch even ordered the construction of a wall between the jury box and the gallery. In all of these actions, he showed how he could work within the existing free press/fair trial framework and still respond to the practicalities of the situation in Denver.

The press tried—unsuccessfully—to use the trial to extend the *Richmond Newspapers* precedent to an unresolved area—does a First Amendment right of access attach to court documents? A coalition of media representatives, organized with little or no consultation with their individual counsel, challenged Judge Matsch's decision to redact several key motions, such as those filed by McVeigh and co-defendant Terry Lynn Nichols, seeking separate trials. The U.S. Court of Appeals for the 10th Circuit, however, affirmed Matsch without deciding whether a right of access applied. The media initiative was probably doomed from the outset and certainly not orchestrated or timed cleverly to enhance the likelihood of success.

Unluckily for the media initiative, Judge Matsch was no oaf or bogeyman. He did not try to interfere unnecessarily with news gathering. Early in the case, he declined to conduct an investigation of alleged leaks of material exchanged between the parties during discovery. And after the *Dallas Morning News* published its account of McVeigh's alleged confession, the judge denied a defense motion to dismiss the case. Instead of browbeating the media for creating a possible disruption of the trial process—a criticism that many in the press itself were willing to make—Matsch reaffirmed free press principles.

"Crimes are prosecuted publicly," he wrote in a March 17, 1997, opinion. "The Constitution commands it. A free and unfettered press is essential to the proper functioning of all democratic institutions, including the people's courts."

Some may think that Matsch was merely playing lip service to the constructive role of the media, given the restrictions he set up in his own courtroom. But even if that were the case, his language returns us to the unifying theme that Chief Justice Burger and Justice Brennan could agree on: that media coverage of trials—even at times messy, chaotic coverage—ultimately is as responsible as anything for public confidence in the criminal justice system. It would be constructive to hear the Supreme Court say so again—and soon.

Bruce W. Sanford, an authority on communications law, is a partner in the Washington, D.C., office of Baker & Hostetler and general counsel to the Society of Professional Journalists. He gratefully acknowledges the assistance of his colleague Bruce D. Brown.

2

Lessons from the Timothy McVeigh Trial I

After Timothy McVeigh was swiftly convicted of the bombing of the Alfred P. Murrah Federal Building in Oklahoma City, commentators couldn't wait to tell us what it all meant.

It meant that a high-profile trial of a defendant accused of a heinous crime can be conducted efficiently when a tough and no-nonsense judge is at the helm. It meant that almost any restriction on public access can be justified if it is ostensibly designed to shield jurors from those who might seek to influence or harm them—or from the news media. It meant that lawyers and other trial participants should be forbidden to say anything about the case outside the courtroom. And most importantly, it meant that to avoid a "media circus," judges should ban cameras from the courtroom.

In other words, the way to guarantee the appearance of a "fair" trial— apparently defined as a trial resulting in the conviction of a defendant who is perceived as guilty by the majority of the American public—is to limit press and public scrutiny of the process as much as possible.

The drafters of the Constitution, who were all too familiar with the legacy of the infamous Court of Star Chamber proceedings, abolished by the British Parliament just 150 years before the ratification of the Bill of Rights, would be stunned by the notion that justice can be done in secret. Yet such simplistic and flawed conclusions from judges, lawyers and journalists who should know better have managed to gut more than 20 years of Supreme Court precedent establishing that the First Amendment requires a presumption that criminal trial proceedings must be open to public scrutiny.

What exactly did Judge Richard Matsch do that so endeared him to legal commentators and the public?

Press reports seem to support the perception that he was business-like and tolerated no posturing in his courtroom. But whatever the significance of Matsch's judicial style, it is far outweighed by the most-cited factor that shaped public opinion about the conduct of the case: the exclusion of cameras, other than a closed-circuit camera forced upon him by congressional fiat to beam the trial to a remote viewing center for victims in Oklahoma City.

Federal rules prohibit cameras in federal criminal trials, and Matsch had no choice but to keep them out. But the absence of cameras virtually guaranteed that the public would be denied the kind of freewheeling, 24-hour coverage by a motley assortment of media that had alternately riveted and repulsed it during the O.J. Simpson trial, and which so many judges, lawyers and print journalists found to be both excessive and distasteful.

In contrast to the front-row seat for the Simpson case available to almost anybody virtually anywhere in the world, the exclusion of cameras meant that only a minuscule segment of the public, supplemented by a handful of reporters, actually saw the proceedings in Denver. Based on the media's secondhand reports, most people seem satisfied that justice was done. It didn't hurt that commentators, most of whom didn't attend the trial, kept reminding everyone how different this trial was from the O.J. Simpson case. Of course, we couldn't know that for sure. However eloquent and enlightening those second- and thirdhand reports might have been, they were no substitute for seeing it ourselves and drawing our own conclusions.

Furthermore, the journalists who did get into the courtroom were hobbled by a variety of restrictions imposed by Matsch in the name of justice: gags on the lawyers, who were forbidden to discuss the case; protective orders closing off pretrial documents; limited access to the jury-selection process and to transcripts of in-camera challenges for cause; impaneling of an "anonymous" jury whose identities were sealed; and the erection of a barricade across one end of the courtroom to obstruct the spectators' view of the individuals who would decide Timothy McVeigh's fate.

With the exception of the barricade, every one of these tactics has been tried by judges in criminal cases in the past. They are frequently and properly struck down as violations of constitutional principles. In those rare cases when they have been upheld on appeal, courts have required the trial judge to demonstrate that a genuine and specific threat to the fair trial rights of the defendant can be averted only through a restriction on the rights of the press and the public.

Generalized concerns about the Sixth Amendment won't suffice. Neither does the sort of free-form anxiety about "juror privacy" that has become epidemic in the last few years. Our criminal courts are supposed to be open to public scrutiny and analysis, and only an overriding interest of the highest order can overcome that presumption.

At least that's the way it is supposed to be. But in the wake of cases like the Rodney King beating trial as well as the O.J. Simpson proceedings, more and more judges are concerned that public perception of the operation of the criminal justice system is in big trouble. They have concluded, not surprisingly, that the way to alter that perception is by controlling the message that the public receives. One way to do that is to shut down access to information.

To his credit, Judge Matsch resisted the impulse to try to restrain what the press had to say about the case, at least overtly. Even he could not ignore the weight of so many years of unswerving Supreme Court precedent declaring that gag orders on the press are presumed unconstitutional. But there is no question that the myriad restrictions on access that he did impose had a significant impact on the ability of the press to report, and for the public to judge for itself, what was going on in that Denver courtroom.

When Judge Matsch's orders were challenged by two coalitions of media organizations in late April 1997, he dismissed the argument that the public had the right to receive information about the proceedings. "What we ought to be trying to do is try to get people to be trusting [of the legal system] rather than cynical," Matsch said, according to the Associated Press.

Expecting the public to "trust" government to carry out the public will, sight unseen, is profoundly at odds with American tradition. It seems particularly inappropriate in a case whose defense turned in no small part on allegations of impropriety in a variety of governmental institutions, not the least of which was the FBI.

It is simply no answer to say that all the attorneys, including McVeigh's lawyers, acceded to many of the restrictions. In the first place, McVeigh's interests are quite distinct from those of the public. For a variety of reasons, criminal defense counsel often agree to or even seek limitations on public access, including exclusion of cameras. They know that their clients are often less than appealing, and they want to control public scrutiny of them as much as possible. They frequently tolerate gag orders on themselves, as long as the trade-off is that the prosecution, which usually operates at a significant public relations advantage, is similarly shackled.

Second, although there is no evidence that it was a factor in the McVeigh case, history is replete with examples of court-appointed defense counsel who were incompetent, or who struck deals with their adversaries that operated to their clients' disadvantage. Sometimes the U.S. Supreme Court has even reversed convictions because of them. Although public oversight can't guarantee that lawyers will do their jobs properly and that the system will be kept honest, it certainly helps.

Which brings us to the greatest irony of all: that in the wake of the O.J. Simpson case, a criminal trial that many people thought represented the worst excesses of our judicial system run amok, the public would actually welcome restrictions on its ability to oversee the McVeigh trial—and would conclude that it was the presence of those restrictions that let justice be done.

In some respects, it is reminiscent of the public reaction to the draconian restraints imposed on the news media by the U.S. military during the Persian Gulf War. That conflict, like the McVeigh trial, was swift, efficient and had a happy resolution. Unlike the disquieting press reports about the Vietnam War, most coverage of the Persian Gulf crisis was upbeat and emphasized the positive. If the news media's ability to independently report was impeded—well, most people thought that those restraints probably contributed to the success of the mission. But only now are the American people finding out the actual success rate of Patriot missiles and the magnitude of exposure of American soldiers to poison gas.

Similarly, an awful lot of people seem to think that the McVeigh trial is the prototype for how justice should be done. But I wonder if they would feel the same if the jury had acquitted McVeigh. I doubt it. But by then, of course, it would have been too late to undo the secrecy provisions that shielded the jury, and the process, from public view.

Jane Kirtley is executive director of the Reporters Committee for Freedom of the Press and edits the Committee's quarterly magazine, The News Media & the Law.

3

Lessons from the Timothy McVeigh Trial II

Andrew Cohen

The playwrights and directors investigated and researched until they found a workable script. Then they selected the best actors and props they could find to tell their story. When they presented their work, they choreographed each scene in the kind of smooth and dramatic fashion that would have made Shakespeare proud. A sad scene here. Some comic relief there. A bit of narrative. A crescendo. A denouement.

The audience appreciated the performance. How do we know? Because the audience, the jury in the case of *United States v. Timothy James McVeigh et al,* applauded the prosecutor's presentation by unanimously convicting the 29-year-old army veteran for his role in the April 19, 1995, bombing of the Alfred P. Murrah building in Oklahoma City. Eleven days later, the same 12 folks sentenced McVeigh to death for murdering and conspiring to murder the 168 people who died in the largest act of domestic terrorism in the nation's history.

It is only slightly hyperbolic to compare the prosecution's presentation at the McVeigh trial with a Broadway show. Sure, trial attorneys always try to present their case in the most entertaining and theatrical fashion possible. But the prosecution's case against McVeigh brought the concept of "trial as art" to a new level, one that is sure to be emulated by lawyers in high-profile cases in the years to come. This, in turn, means that journalists will have to be particularly vigilant if they are to separate attorneys' artifice from real news.

The media were there, of course. Fresh from the Simpson circuses in southern California, they descended upon the federal courthouse in Denver half expecting another courtroom brawl leading to a dubious acquittal. What they found instead was a legal rout, a surprisingly one-sided trial if there ever was one. So, in addition to reporting on the usual suspects in a high-profile case—who won, who lost, whose witness suffered a meltdown on the stand, which attorney stood up to the judge—reporters covering the McVeigh trial also ended up exploring the prosecution's creative onslaught. Story after story noted the polished strength of the government's case and how "dramatic" and "emotional" the prosecution's testimony seemed to be playing out in court.

Nothing wrong with that because in this particular case the government's onslaught happened to be true, and the creativity sure looked newsworthy. The media simply told it like they saw it. And for the most part they told it well and accurately.

The real takeaway question from the McVeigh trial, however, is whether it created such a new paradigm for high-profile cases—with entertainment, quick movement, drama and dazzling presentation—that it will cause reporters to focus on style over substance the next time the whole world comes to watch an important trial. On the cynical side of the street, it's probably also worth asking whether lead federal prosecutor Joseph Hartzler and company sculpted their presentation with the media in mind to ensure good press and satisfy members of the various victims' rights groups that proliferated after the bombing.

First, though, let's take a closer look at how the prosecution choreographed its victory. The government's case was as smooth and theatrical as the media said it was because that's the way prosecutors had planned it. Hartzler told me after the trial that his team focused on ensuring sustained "engagement" with the jury by "scripting" the case so that it unfolded "very much like live theatre." Shakespeare Goes to Court, you might say, from the federal prosecutor who studied drama and literature in college before heading off to law school. What "engagement" and "scripting" really mean, of course, is that the prosecution intentionally established and maintained a feverish emotional pitch throughout the presentation of the 18-day trial.

Pick a day, any day. One day it was one of the government's star witnesses, come to tell the eerie tale of McVeigh's bombing plans. The next day it might be a scientific witness, come to read the forensic tea leaves, which pointed inexorably to McVeigh. Next it might be one of the many sad survivors of the bombing, come to tell her tale of woe. And if it wasn't the witnesses themselves, it was the way prosecutors arranged their order. If the jurors appeared to be getting sleepy because of technical, scientific testimony, prosecutors trotted out a survivor whose testimony woke everyone up and got them good and sad and indignant. But if things were getting a little too morose, prosecutors relieved the stress by bringing an eyewitness or an FBI agent to the stand. Nothing like the testimony of an FBI agent to put the brakes on emotions in a courtroom.

Here's just one of many examples of the "dramatic moment" prosecutors achieved during the trial. On May 13, McVeigh attorney Stephen Jones finished a grueling cross-examination of the government's star witness, Michael Fortier. Jones had damaged Fortier's credibility by portraying him as a drug-using, fame-seeking liar. Some prosecutors might have tried to rehabilitate Fortier by rehashing Jones' line of questioning point by point. This might have worked—but it also might have reinforced Fortier's many bad points. Hartzler instead asked Fortier only about a half dozen questions. Do you remember driving around the remains of the Murrah building with the feds after the bombing? Yes. Had you heard any news about a particular alley? No. You told us about an alley, didn't you? Yes. Do you know that the FBI found a Ryder truck key in that alley? No.

End of redirect questioning. Next witness? An FBI agent who identified the key that apparently started the truck that blew up the building. In only 10 minutes of scripted, near-palpable drama, the prosecution had succeeded in re-establishing Fortier's credibility, neutralizing a central defense theme (that Fortier's story was based on media reports) and introducing into the case another damaging piece of evidence against McVeigh. There were probably a dozen ways the feds could have gotten that key into evidence, but they chose a purely dramatic way to do it.

Why? Not because it made for good copy. Or because prosecutors felt they needed to win over the hearts and minds of the American public by manipulating the media. Hartzler, in fact, laughed aloud before emphatically answering "No" when I asked him whether he had scripted his case with the media in mind. That happens in politics, of course, but it doesn't really happen during a trial. Once a trial begins, remember, the only "constituents" lawyers normally care about are the judge and jury because only the judge and jury decide their client's fate. So the answer to our cynical question is: Relax, the media were not the target of any sinister manipulation by the government during the McVeigh trial.

The McVeigh script was designed as dramatically as it was not for the media's sake but because lawyers are becoming more and more convinced that they need drama and entertainment in an age when attention spans have been diminished by television. And keeping the jury's attention can be half the battle when you are trying to win a long, complex circumstantial case like the government's case against McVeigh.

It's a legal lesson prosecutors in the O.J. Simpson criminal trial never quite got into their heads—and a lesson the McVeigh prosecutors never forgot.

Since there is no law prohibiting lawyers from presenting their evidence theatrically, trial reporters therefore are likely to see more and more of these "dramatic moments" during even the most tedious of trials. Direct and cross-examinations likely will become shorter and more focused, and videotapes, audiotapes and overhead presentations will continue to grow in popularity. Meanwhile, jurors will come to expect lawyers to choreograph a tight production à la McVeigh and will be disappointed when they don't get one. There is nothing inherently wrong with all this, so long as judges have the spine and the intelligence to ensure that trials don't become soap operas at the expense of justice. Most judges are up to the task, fortunately, so there's no need to worry just yet.

Reporters working under this new trial paradigm will have to be especially vigilant to ensure that they can recognize and separate the sizzle from the steak. They must be willing and able to distinguish the true "dramatic moment," one in which the lawyer effectively uses drama to prove an important legal point, from just plain showbiz, where a lawyer tries to bamboozle the judge or jury with a legal sleight of hand. This means having the ability to avoid getting caught up in the drama at the expense of the evidence: Six entertaining witnesses, for example, might make for great copy and mean absolutely nothing to the judge or jury. It means knowing when a lawyer is shouting because he has no case or when a lawyer is whispering because he knows he's about to unleash the punch line. And it means knowing how all this choreography at trial reflects the talent and ambitions and strategies of the lawyers presenting it.

The McVeigh trial media were generally uncritical of the prosecution's case because there was little to be critical about. The real test will come the next time lawyers go artsy and entertaining without the evidence to back it up.

Andrew Cohen is a Denver lawyer and journalist. He is a legal consultant for CBS Radio and a legal analyst on the Oklahoma City bombing trials for Fox News, Tribune Broadcasting Co. and the Denver Post.

4

The Reardon Ruckus

Richard M. Schmidt Jr. and Kevin M. Goldberg

Born of tragedy, its existence marked by conflicts that reduced its impact, the Reardon Report sought "methods of preserving and strengthening the right to a fair trial without abridging freedom of speech and of the press." Despite short-term failure, the report set off 30 years of dialogue between the press and the bar. If the two parties have rarely been in complete agreement about what to do, at least their commitment to keep talking has saved journalists and the courts from destructive estrangement.

The roots of the Reardon Report lie in the Warren Commission's investigation of the Kennedy assassination and its concern that reporting about Lee Harvey Oswald would have made it impossible to give him a fair trial. The Warren Commission called upon representatives of the news media, the bar and law enforcement to work together to establish ethical standards for reporting. Ideally, these standards would prevent interference with court proceedings and pending criminal investigations while reserving the right to a fair trial.

The American Bar Association accepted the challenge. Six advisory committees were appointed; one of them, chaired by Paul C. Reardon, associate justice of the Supreme Judicial Court of Massachusetts, covered "fair trial and free press." Reardon's committee was directed to consider the impact of news reporting on the administration of criminal justice. Its members included distinguished judges, lawyers and legal educators— but no journalists. That absence would later haunt the committee.

For one month, in 20 metropolitan centers, the Reardon Committee conducted a content analysis of major newspapers and sent questionnaires to police officials, prosecutors, defense attorneys, judges and editors. The Committee determined that in 80 instances, a suspect's record of prior convictions or arrests and indictments was disseminated between an arrest and a trial. In all but seven of those 80 instances, the source of information was the local police department.

In October 1966, the Committee released its report. It concluded that in virtually every one of the 80 cases it studied, restraint by public officials—including the "willingness to wait until the danger to the fairness to the criminal process had passed to release certain information or to state opinions"—would have substantially reduced or eliminated the threat to a fair trial.

The diagnosis inspired the prescription: restraints on lawyers, law enforcement officers and court personnel to regulate the release of information or opinion about a criminal trial from the time a suspect was subject to an arrest warrant until a plea bargain or completion of the trial. The report also proposed to prohibit reporting on the defendant's confessions, admissions or statements, reporting on the defendant's performance on any examinations or tests and reporting on the identity, testimony or credibility of prospective witnesses.

Finally, the Reardon Report recommended that the defendant in a criminal trial could move that all or part of any pretrial hearing could be closed to the public—with a presumption in favor of granting such a motion. In effect, a defendant could close important parts of a criminal trial to the public unless the press could show an overriding need to report on the case.

Criticism of the report in the press rose to a crescendo, much to the surprise and concern of the ABA. Journalists, noting that 90 percent of all criminal cases are disposed of before trial, feared that allowing the closure of pretrial hearings would destroy their ability to report on important criminal cases. The press also felt that the remaining 10 percent would receive ineffective coverage because the proposed limitations would amount to prior restraint.

If one envisions this effort to balance fair trial/free press as a school-yard seesaw, then fair trial was the 800-pound gorilla to the free press's 98-pound weakling. But the press brought down the 800-pound gorilla with an old school-yard trick—it jumped off the seesaw. While the Reardon Committee expressed its sincere desire to accommodate the rights of the press, the press fired a steady barrage of critical articles and commentary at the Committee, accusing it of inadequate research.

A glimmer of the prospect of a solution appeared in 1969, when Norman Isaacs, executive editor of the Louisville, Ky., *Courier Journal* and *Louisville Times* became president of the American Society of Newspaper

Editors. Deciding that action had to be taken to "cool the rhetoric" being hurled by both sides in the Reardon ruckus, he met with Bernard Segal of Philadelphia, who had just become president of the ABA. ASNE and the ABA began to work together toward an accommodation.

One of the first steps taken by the ABA was to create the Legal Advisory Committee on Fair Trial-Free Press, whose first action was to encourage voluntary guidelines for the bar and media. Because guidelines would not have the force of law, a reporter who violated them would not be sanctioned by the courts—although his or her conduct could be brought to the attention of others in his or her profession. In this formula, contrary to the Reardon Report, self-regulation would take the place of court sanctions.

The ABA asked each state bar association to create a fair trial-free press committee to represent the legal profession and to consult with media groups. Forty-four states complied. At the same time, many editors developed guidelines for their own staffs.

ASNE's own press/bar committee met with the ABA committees in October of 1969 to plan joint voluntary state and local bar committees on free press and fair trial. While the two groups concluded that "communication" and "education" were needed, the ABA moved ahead on the only area it had the power to regulate—the Reardon Report's legal code applying to lawyer conduct. Subsequently, the American Newspaper Publishers Association (now Newspaper Association of America) formed a special task force to work with the ABA and invited editors and other press groups to join them.

Despite such steps toward cooperation, two major court cases demonstrated the complexity of relations between the press and the bar when it comes to establishing guidelines for the press.

In 1975, in western Nebraska, a man was accused of murdering six members of a family in a grizzly set of killings with revolting sexual overtones. A suspect was quickly seized, and he admitted to many of the charges against him. The trial judge, citing the Nebraska Bar-Press Guidelines, issued a "gag order" that limited reports on public pretrial proceedings. Many citizens attended these proceedings, however, and then related accounts of them throughout their community.

Barred from reporting on events that were common knowledge, the Nebraska press respected the "gag order" but appealed it to the next higher level of the judiciary. When the Nebraska appellate courts failed to take emergency action, the press appealed to Justice Harry A. Blackmun of the U.S. Supreme Court. As the circuit justice, Blackmun was charged with overseeing the proper functioning of the courts in the 8th Circuit of the United States, which included Nebraska.

Blackmun declared that the delays by the lower courts exceeded tolerable limits for gag orders. Moreover, he stated that the most troublesome aspect of the District Court's gag order was its wholesale incorporation of the Nebraska Bar-Press Guidelines, which were conceived as voluntary agreements between the press and bar. The very guidelines that had been drawn up to ensure less judicial intervention in news gathering and more balanced coverage of trials were being used to muzzle the press.

The Nebraska Supreme Court later agreed with Blackmun's determination that voluntary press-bar guidelines mean "voluntary," and the guidelines could not be made mandatory by court authority. It overturned the portion of the trial judge's order that forced the press to abide by these guidelines. Subsequently the full Supreme Court, in the case of *Nebraska Press Association v. Stuart,* approvingly noted efforts to develop voluntary guidelines for courts, lawyers and the press—but stopped short of declaring that these guidelines could never be made mandatory.

For both the press and the bar, *Nebraska Press Association* brought home the dangers of litigation. The press realized that even when it wins the battle it often loses the war: An appellate court may grant a right of access to the press in a general sense, but it may come long after the pretrial proceeding at issue is completed. Judges were reminded that litigation over the rights of the press during a trial forces attention away from the overriding question of whether or not the defendant is guilty. Judges were also put in mind of the public interest in full, free and timely reporting on criminal trials.

The 1981 case of *Federated Publications, Inc. v. Swedburg,* which grew out of proceedings around a trial for attempted murder, sharpened the discussion of guidelines. In a response to a motion from the defense, the trial court ruled that reporters could attend a pretrial hearing only if they signed an agreement to abide by the Washington Bar-Press Guidelines. While some journalists signed the agreement and attended the hearing, *Federated Publications* called the ruling an unconstitutional prior restraint on the press and appealed.

The Washington state Supreme Court held that press access to pretrial hearings may be conditioned upon reporters' agreement to abide by "voluntary" state-press guidelines. Such guidelines, the court reasoned, are not prior restraints but reasonable limitations that accommodate the interests of both press and public. In 1982, the Supreme Court declined to hear the appeal of *Federated Publications.*

Angry press groups around the country registered their response: If voluntary guidelines were going to become mandatory, there would be no further efforts to develop them. The cooperative efforts that had existed in many states turned into shouting matches.

Federated Publications established that reporters' access to court proceedings may be conditioned on adherence to voluntary guidelines. In such circumstances, reporters have realized that fighting the bar is not as productive as working with the legal profession to obtain maximum access to court proceedings from the start.

Since the Reardon Report, three decades of discussions between lawyers and journalists have fallen short of producing absolute agreement on free press/fair trial. But in many local communities this conversation, despite some strained moments, has fostered strong personal relationships among members of the press and members of the bar. Out of these connections grows the hope that voluntary cooperation between bar and media groups, now effective at the national level, will once again function at the state and local levels.

Court battles between lawyers and journalists are a diminishing occurrence today because guidelines for fair trial/free press are being written with an eye toward mutual satisfaction. The press has also recognized that litigation, even in victory, is costly and time consuming.

As a starting point for standards regarding press-bar relations, the Reardon Report proposed to favor the bar and stifle journalists. Since the Reardon ruckus, both sides have met in the middle—with many positive results. Court personnel understand what information is important to reporters and how to meet the needs of reporters without generating prejudicial publicity. The press has gained a knowledge of court procedures and consequently can be fairer and more accurate in its reporting.

The benefit of the dialogue that has flowed from the Reardon Report is not that lawyers and journalists have always agreed on what to do about free press/fair trial. They have, however, agreed what *not* to do— namely, impose prior restraints. In the contentious discussions between the press and the bar over the delicate balance between freedom of the press and the right to a fair trial, this is modest but significant progress.

Richard M. Schmidt Jr. is a partner and Kevin M. Goldberg is an associate in the Washington, D.C., law firm of Cohn and Marks. They are legal counsel to the American Society of Newspaper Editors.

5

The Thicket of Rules North of the Border

G. Stuart Adam

American journalists—not to mention a substantial number of their Canadian colleagues—were astonished in July 1993 to discover that they could not report the evidence presented at the short trial of the notorious Karla Homolka.

The trial had attracted wide publicity throughout Canada and the United States. Homolka and her even more notorious husband, Paul Bernardo, had been accused of collaborating in a deadly sex game that led to the rape and murder of two teenagers in 1991 and 1992. But a judge prevented the most gruesome and incriminating facts from circulating until Bernardo was tried for first-degree murder in 1995.

Welcome to Canada, where the thicket of rules designed to protect judicial proceedings is a good deal more dense than it is south of the border!

Think of it. The Canadian Criminal Code contains a provision prohibiting jurors from revealing what was said in the jury room. Another confers on judges the power to ban reports of evidence presented in bail hearings. And the common law crime of contempt can be used to prevent a journalist from reporting evidence heard in one trial if it is believed it might prejudice the result of another.

It was common law that provided the authority for the judge's action in the Homolka trial. In the period leading up to it, Homolka had distanced herself from Bernardo, pleaded guilty to manslaughter and agreed to testify for the prosecution at his trial.

Enter Mr. Justice Francis Kovacs of the Ontario Court of Justice. Just as the manslaughter trial was getting under way, he issued the banning order and justified it principally on the grounds that premature publication of many of the important and incriminating facts might prejudice Bernardo's right to a fair trial even though he knew it would be many months before the trial would be scheduled.

Some commentators continue to argue that Mr. Justice Kovacs should not have issued the ban, but few would disagree with the proposition that his actions were, well, Canadian. The question that arises naturally in the wake of such a decision is, Why do Canadian judges act that way? Are they not reasonable? Do they not understand democracy and freedom?

The answer takes some explaining since the practices at issue reflect a truly distinctive legal and political culture. If Canada is to Americans a foreign country, its foreign-ness is to be found in the British character of its political practices, its public institutions and its legal system.

The formal authority of the state looms larger in Canada and in Britain than it does in the United States. The British North America Act, originally a statute of the Parliament at Westminster, provided the foundation for Canada's constitutional order when it was passed in 1867. It conferred on the Parliament in Ottawa a general power to "make Laws for the Peace, Order and good Government of Canada."

That phrase more or less says it all. The spirit of the British North America Act was and continues to be that government is the source and custodian of the social order. There is no phrase in it celebrating individual freedom—no "life, liberty, and the pursuit of happiness" providing a starting point for collective life.

So in constitutional disputes that pit the freedom of individuals and institutions against other broad social values, the social values are likely to receive equivalent or, occasionally, greater weight. Examples of these values may be found in legislation intended to protect children from inappropriate advertising or women from the effects of pornography or minorities from hateful speech.

The rules governing the judicial process fall into this broad category of a privileged social value. The Canadian reason for the protections conferred on these rules is clear and simple to articulate: Justice requires it.

This belief is enshrined in the constitutional regime. The Canadian Constitution now has two fundamental parts: the British North America Act, renamed the Constitution Act of 1867, and the Canadian Charter of Rights and Freedoms, or Constitution Act of 1982. The first embodies the idea, as it says in the preamble, that Canada will have a Constitution "similar in Principle to that of the United Kingdom." The second, which entered our constitutional history late in the day, added an American-style dimension with what amounted to a Bill of Rights and judicial review. It was widely celebrated when it was introduced by the government of Pierre Elliott Trudeau in 1982.

Among the celebrants were journalists who believed that at last they had something akin to a First Amendment. They believed they would benefit from the declaration in Section 2(b) of the Charter that says the freedoms "of thought, belief, opinion and expression, including freedom of the press and other media of communication" are fundamental and guaranteed.

But there was an unanticipated catch. Section 1 of the very same Charter qualifies the freedoms it guarantees by saying that they can be limited for strong reasons. Section 1 says that the rights and freedoms are "subject only to such reasonable limits prescribed by law as can be demonstrably justified in a free and democratic society."

That declaration sets in motion a complex method for testing legal limits on such freedoms, including media freedom. It also provides opportunities for the continuation of the judicial practices established before the Charter.

So the change in method, while it made a difference in some of the law's domains, did not create a true revolution in the way the media would cover the courts. Tradition continued to play an important role.

But it should not be assumed that anti-democratic impulses were at work. For a long time, the assumption of the constitutional regime has been that the media are essential to the administration of justice. The Charter reflects this understanding in Section 11(d), which says that an accused person "has a right to be presumed innocent until proven guilty according to law in a fair and public hearing by an independent and impartial tribunal." The trial must be public. So the courts are open and journalists have free access to them.

There is a considerable amount of judicial reflection on this openness principle. Mr. Justice Peter Cory said in the Supreme Court of Canada in *Edmonton Journal v. Alberta* that "[d]iscussion of court cases and constructive criticism of court proceedings is dependent upon the receipt by the public of information as to what transpired in court. Practically speaking, this information can only be obtained from the newspapers or other media."

Not quite poetic; not the vigor of Justice William Brennan in *Times v. Sullivan* (or, indeed, other Canadian decisions on freedom of the press). But the points are made in this and other judgments that in a democratic society the courts are public institutions, they must be subject to public scrutiny, and such scrutiny can only be achieved through reporting by journalists.

So the openness principle is axiomatic and well understood in Canada, just as it is in the United States. Conceived this way, even Mr. Justice Kovacs believed, as he embargoed the evidence in the Homolka trial, that the media facilitate justice. Publicity is seen in Canada as a means in a system in which justice is the end. But the publicity can be regulated in the name of the formal value placed on justice and the rules intended to guarantee that justice is done. In short, publicity is a necessary component in the system, but it should not interfere with the administration of justice.

Since the charter was introduced, the media have challenged its regulations on many occasions by invoking the freedom of expression provisions in Section 2(b). Sometimes they have succeeded. More often they have not because, in a strictly technical sense, the rules have received protection from the limiting principles in Section 1.

An instructive example of the way in which the freedom and limiting provisions of the Charter interact occurred in the case of Cathy Squires, a reporter with the Canadian Broadcasting Corp. Squires was prosecuted and convicted in 1989 for filming inside a courthouse contrary to a provision of the Ontario Judicature Act. When the matter was heard in the Ontario Court of Appeal, Squires argued that she was wrongly convicted because the prohibition in the act violated her Charter-endowed rights to freedom of expression. A majority in the court agreed that while the provision diminished her freedom, the statute was nevertheless constitutional because it was aimed at achieving the higher social value of protecting the integrity of the judicial system.

The basis for the judgment was bound up with a traditional view—one can hear British judges speaking—that the "fair and impartial administration of justice requires a calm, dignified atmosphere." Decorum and order are considered essential to the administration of justice and fair trials. "Peace, Order and good Government."

So Squires could report, pencil in hand, as she pleased. Courts are open. But she could not film the participants even in the corridors outside the courtroom.

Except under the rarest of circumstances, cameras and video recorders are not allowed in Canadian trial courts. Oddly, they are allowed in a couple of appeal courts including the Supreme Court of Canada, but, as Robert Martin has remarked in his book, *Media Law,* nobody "seems to care seriously about whether journalists record proceedings before appellate courts, largely because these proceedings are not very interesting."

The provision in the Ontario Judicature Act and its successor, the Courts of Justice Act, is an example of a statutory rule limiting media freedom. There are others. Under the Federal Criminal Code, judges at preliminary hearings may, and usually do, issue orders prohibiting the publication of evidence. The bans on evidence at such hearings are discretionary and depend on motions by counsel. Prohibitions on reporting confessions are automatic and all Canadian reporters should know it.

Curiously, a reported case that illustrates how the discretionary rules apply in preliminary hearings involves a U.S. journalist. In February 1982, Beurmond Banville, on assignment for the *Bangor* (Maine) *Daily News,* attended a hearing in Edmunston, New Brunswick. The presiding judge, in response to a request from the defense, ordered that the evidence not be published. Banville ignored the order and published his account the next day.

Largely because copies of the *News* circulated in New Brunswick and the judge believed the reports could influence potential jurors, Banville was convicted and fined. On appeal, he received an absolute discharge and didn't have to pay the fine. But the relevant provision of the Criminal Code continues in force despite Banville's attempt to challenge it under the freedom of expression provisions of the Charter.

That there is very little case law involving preliminary hearing suggests that, for the most part, Canadian journalists comply with the law's provisions. The Canadian reason for such bans—discretionary and compulsory—is that preliminary hearings are not trials; they are conducted to determine if there is sufficient evidence to hold a trial. Thus the reporting is largely postponed until a trial commences or the accused is discharged.

The bans that mark preliminary hearings are statutory applications of an ancient and broad common law principle expressed by the sub judice rule that was invoked by the judge in the Homolka case. The fundamental idea of that rule is that once a person is formally accused of a crime, the matter is before a court and subject to its authority.

According to the principles of sub judice, journalists are not supposed to report items of evidence before they are heard in court. The rule is designed to prevent trials by media. Nevertheless, except in very rare cases like Homolka-Bernardo, fair and accurate reporting of the proceedings in open court is unimpaired once the trial begins.

For similar reasons, journalists in Canada are prohibited from reporting proceedings when members of a jury are asked to leave the court so that a judge can decide if contentious facts are admissible. The journalists may remain, but they may not report what is said while the jury is out. The theory is that the jurors, who are rarely sequestered, might hear such evidence on radio or television or read it in a newspaper when they go home at night.

The sub judice rule is not limited to reporting. Under the principle that says the place for trials is the courts, journalists can be prohibited from publishing commentary on issues in a trial if the commentary is intended to promote a particular result or might otherwise prejudice it.

The rule leads occasionally to unpredictable events. For example, in 1992, it was used to justify an injunction postponing the Canadian Broadcasting Corp. from broadcasting *The Boys of St. Vincent,* a docudrama on the sexual abuse of young males by priests. A trial of a real priest accused of similar behavior was about to start in Montreal, and the court held that broadcasting the docudrama might prejudice the outcome.

The injunction was contested and amended so that the broadcast could be shown immediately outside Ontario and Quebec, and it was finally set aside when the Supreme Court reviewed it. But the principle survives—namely, that an article, docudrama, editorial or column that might prejudice the outcome of a trial by jury may be subject to the sub judice rule.

The theory of the sub judice rule explains a substantial portion of the law to which journalists must bow when they report trials. But there are some other statutory rules arising out of other kinds of policy objectives contained in statutes that the courts have recognized as reasonable limits. For example, judges hearing sexual assault cases must order journalists not to disclose the identity of victims if either the prosecution or the defense asks for a ban. The public policy justification, sanctioned by the premises of Section 1 of the Charter, is a belief that female victims will be more willing to report sexual assaults if the courts confer upon them the comfort of privacy.

Similarly, under the terms of the Young Offenders Act, juveniles accused of crimes cannot be identified in the media because public policy on juvenile criminals is intended to rehabilitate rather than punish. Judges have agreed that the legislative intent of the act is a reasonable limit on media freedom.

So it goes in Canada.

It is easy to say where the differences in Canadian and American practices come from. We started and stayed for a long time with the British. The effects are clearly discernible in the degree to which respect for the judiciary is demanded, orderliness is considered a primary good and the integrity of the judicial process is carefully protected. But the system is still democratic. The courts are open, and the judiciary and judicial process are subject to continuous commentary and reporting.

This is not to say that there is not a price to be paid for the constraints imposed upon journalists. For example, their capacity to collect news as it happens is clearly diminished by the spirit, not to mention the applications, of the common law sub judice rule and by parallel statutory constraints.

American journalists clearly find such constraints unwarranted. The *Washington Post, Newsweek,* the *Detroit Free Press* and the *Buffalo Evening News* were among the U.S. media organizations that ignored the wishes of the judge in the Homolka case and published details of the trial. No Canadian media organization followed suit, although they reported that the Americans had broken the embargo.

As far as I know, there were no cross-border citations for contempt— no Banville appeared in a Canadian court this time. There was no need for such an action since the judge's intent was to preserve the possibility that a jury could be found from a pool of individuals who had not been prejudiced by the early disclosure of incriminating facts. It's not all that difficult to locate Canadians who haven't read such publications. Nor is it all that difficult to find Canadians who don't consult the news groups on the Internet where some of the embargoed evidence against Homolka circulated illegally.

In the meantime, sensational cases in Canada are less sensational and less likely to produce the circuses that marked several American trials in recent years—most notably the trial of O.J. Simpson. Very little of the commentary that was seen on television or recorded in books and the press even before the trial began could ever have been circulated if O.J. had been a Canadian citizen and tried in Canada. But the details of the evidence would have been reported as they were presented in court in the belief that justice must be done in the glare of publicity.

G. Stuart Adam, vice president (academic) of Carleton University in Canada and former director of its School of Journalism, is co-author of A Sourcebook of Canadian Media Law.

II

Cameras in the Courts

"For advocates of cameras in courts, an unfunny thing happened on the way to the millennium—the televised O.J. Simpson trial."

—Fred Graham

6

Doing Justice with Cameras in the Courts

Fred Graham

For advocates of cameras in courts, an unfunny thing happened on the way to the millennium—the televised O.J. Simpson trial.

In the early years of the 1990s, television coverage of trials expanded rapidly. The concerns of some lawyers and judges that cameras would adversely affect trials were rarely borne out in the growing number of cases that were televised, and it appeared that the camera had made its case.

But within two years of the debacle in Judge Lance Ito's courtroom, the rush to televised judgment had stalled. The federal courts, after a successful three-year experiment with TV in court, had rejected camera coverage. California and New York had backed away from their earlier full acceptance of cameras in courts. And virtually without exception, judges across the country presiding over important cases rejected TV coverage of those trials.

Another example of killing the messenger that brought unpleasant news? Partly, yes. But there is more to it than that. It does seem that some of the public repugnance over the unseemly Simpson trial has been turned against the courtroom camera that was a link in the multimedia extravaganza that took place. But beyond that, it now appears that a fundamental unresolved issue about the role of the courts had been festering beneath the surface of the cameras-in-courts debate, one that is being forced into the open by the Simpson backlash.

That issue is, How much importance should the judicial system give to doing justice in public? Is the sole function of the courts to dispense justice between competing parties, so that any proposed measures to inform the public should be rejected if they might conceivably affect a trial? Or is opening the courts to the public a value in itself, which should be accommodated unless there is some showing that the quality of justice would be diminished?

Where these questions have been raised by the print media, the U.S. Supreme Court has invoked the free-press guarantee of the First Amendment and has required openness under almost all circumstances. But because the Supreme Court does not extend the free-press guarantee fully to television, the judges in the states have been left to decide, usually as a matter of judicial policy, how much value to accord to TV access.

In most states, the state Supreme Court has the authority to decide as a general matter whether cameras will be admitted. If the state high court approves camera coverage, it usually gives the states' trial judges discretion to admit or exclude cameras at any given trial.

Under this arrangement, a pattern of steadily increasing camera approval developed. The low point had been the 1965 U.S. Supreme Court decision in the case of *Billie Sol Estes v. Texas,* in which the Court ruled against TV coverage of a trial conducted in a circus atmosphere but did not say that TV coverage was inherently unconstitutional. As television cameras became smaller, quieter and less noticeable, a few states began to permit TV coverage. In 1981, the Supreme Court was finally called upon to decide if TV coverage of criminal trials violates defendants' rights when there is no circuslike atmosphere, and the Court ruled, in *Chandler v. Florida,* that it does not.

After that, courts across the country rapidly opened their doors to TV coverage. By the early 1990s, almost every state allowed cameras in some judicial proceedings, and about two-thirds of the states permitted cameras freely into trial courts, subject to the judges' discretion. Some trial judges never allowed them, but that number was dwindling.

Then, in 1995, came the O.J. Simpson trial, followed by a "Simpson backlash" that had a curious impact on thinking within the judiciary.

There's a story about a rooster who crowed at dawn each day and came to believe he made the sun come up. The rooster had it backward, of course, and that's what happened to the judges who concluded that because a television camera was present in Judge Ito's unruly courtroom, it caused the disarray of the Simpson trial. A more logical conclusion would have been that Judge Ito lost control of his courtroom, and the camera permitted the world to see the ugly spectacle that resulted.

As time has passed since the Simpson debacle, it has become apparent that the judiciary is getting something else backward—judges are concluding that because the Simpson trial was a high-profile case, TV cameras should be banned from other high-interest trials.

This is not just wrongheaded—it's counter to the public interest.

It seems to be fostering a new judicial assumption that if a trial is interesting to the public, by definition it is one they should not be permitted to see. The result could be that the trials most likely to inform the American people about matters of public importance will not be available to them.

How did judicial thinking on cameras in courts become so self-contradictory?

The process began when Los Angeles Superior Court Judge Hiroshi Fujisaki banned cameras from the O.J. Simpson civil trial, and then, in his usual firm manner, conducted a dignified trial.

In hindsight, it is obvious that the elements that made the Ito trial a shambles were absent from the civil case. The raucous race issue was kept out of the trial; the lawyers were professional and restrained; and Judge Fujisaki demonstrated that he would have run a proper trial under any circumstances. It seems likely that if Judge Fujisaki had permitted camera coverage, the trial would have proceeded in a decorous manner, and the "Simpson backlash" against cameras would have ended there.

But as it happened, after the debacle of the first Simpson trial, virtually every judge presiding over a high-visibility trial found some reason to ban cameras. It happened in the South Carolina child-drowning trial of Susan Smith; in the Texas trial of the accused killer of singing star Selena; in the New Jersey child-murder trial of Jesse Timmendequas, whose crime inspired "Megan's law"; in the California murder trial of Richard Allen Davis, whose murder of Polly Klaas inspired the "three strikes you're out" laws; and even in the second trial of the Menendez brothers.

None of these judges gave an up-front rationale that they were banning TV coverage because there was high public interest in the trial. But by mid-1997, the pattern was so well established that essentially that reason was given by the judge who banned cameras from the trial of the Pakistani man accused of killing two CIA employees outside the agency's Langley, Va., headquarters. "It is the very high-profile nature of this case," Judge J. Howe Brown explained, "that makes it unique and makes cameras inappropriate."

Finally, the untelevised Timothy McVeigh bombing trial, conducted by Federal District Judge Richard Matsch with efficiency and dignity, seemed to authenticate the growing judicial notion that important trials shouldn't be on TV.

The irony is that almost all of the 47 states that allow camera coverage of court proceedings first conducted an experiment or study showing that cameras are not harmful, and those findings are still valid. Some included detailed studies indicating that cameras did not adversely affect the behavior of judges, attorneys and others. Yet with no empirical evidence to alter those findings, judges are carving out a "high-profile" exception to the laws allowing cameras in court.

The most frequent reason given is that televising high-interest cases may upset witnesses or jurors. But there's no evidence that anybody who would be unnerved by a camera wouldn't be equally unstrung by the intensity of a major case with the courtroom crammed with print reporters and the cameras waiting outside.

In fact, no coherent rationale has been given for creating a "high-profile" exemption, and cameras are allowed in routine cases as fully as ever.

Why is this happening?

With some judges, the real motivation for barring cameras from big cases may be "Itophobia"—fear of appearing as inept as Judge Ito, with the multitudes watching. Others genuinely believe that the misbehavior of the lawyers in the Simpson case was stimulated by the cameras—not by Judge Ito's lack of control—and that high-profile cases encourage lawyers to showboat. Some judges and lawyers are also horrified that another widely watched televised trial might again show the public the system's warts, writ large, as in the Simpson case.

There is also a subtle sentiment among some judges that allowing themselves to be seen on television is injudicious and unseemly, even if it doesn't harm the trial. The unspoken corollary of this mindset is that those judges who do permit cameras are, perhaps, show-offs.

This feeling is quietly nourished by the example of the U.S. Supreme Court—which refuses to permit TV coverage of its proceedings, even though this would be immensely instructive to the American public and couldn't possibly affect the outcome of any case. The justices have never been moved to give their reasons for refusing, but stray comments by a few justices suggest that they do not wish to be recognized in public, and they fear that being seen on TV might diminish the lofty mystique of the Court.

This mindset may be the core of the problem. Some judges appear to place no value on the opportunity for the public to see justice in progress—so that any countervailing factor, however questionable and speculative, tips the scales toward banning TV coverage.

Too many judges seem almost oblivious to the long tradition of public viewing of trials in America, and to the powerful reasons for it. Our nation inherited the tradition from England, where in the 16th century all the townspeople were actually required to attend trials, and later, when that proved a burden, the rule was relaxed and all were encouraged to attend. In that spirit, the early American courtrooms were huge, theaterlike set-ups where, as Justice Holmes put it, "every citizen should be able to satisfy himself with his own eyes" that justice was being conducted fairly. Thus the reason for the tradition of public viewing was to validate the judicial system itself. As Chief Justice Warren Burger put it, this openness was "an indispensable attribute of an Anglo-American trial," because it "gave assurance that the proceedings were conducted fairly to all concerned, and it discouraged perjury, the misconduct of participants, and decisions based on secret bias or partiality."

But in modern America, there are additional reasons for public viewing of trials: It is an unparalleled way to inform the public about vital issues of governance and everyday life. Present-day Americans are often isolated and poorly informed about their government and their neighbors. Much of what they know they get from television.

For instance, people could learn valuable lessons from viewing the trial of accused Langley killer Mir Aimal Kansi. Why was he so embittered against the CIA? Was the agency's security adequate? Did the government violate his rights in bringing him back for trial? Even if so, was it justified?

Consider what millions of Americans might have learned from watching the Oklahoma City bombing trial on television: In human terms, the story was told of young men's resentment of the powerful government, their outrage over the Waco, Texas, killings, their paranoia, their lack of moral restraint and the capacity of a very few of them to do great harm.

Witness middle-profile trials that were televised, despite the Simpson backlash: the latest assisted-suicide trial of Dr. Jack Kevorkian and the case of two Army skinheads from Fort Bragg, N.C., accused of the racist murders of two blacks. The Kevorkian trial exposed serious questions as to whether the woman who committed suicide might have felt improper family pressures to do so. The skinhead trial revealed an astonishing ignorance by the Army of racist (and, by the way, sexual) activity in its barracks.

Even run-of-the-mill trials have a way of revealing truths about contemporary America that the public could scarcely learn in any other way. Some samples from trials televised in recent years: In a New Haven, Conn., murder trial, witnesses told how a pool of weapons was maintained by inner-city youths for use in committing crimes and settling scores. When a Massachusetts high school athlete was brought to trial for the alleged jealousy murder of his girlfriend, admiring high school girls cut classes to support him from the courtroom gallery. Eight witnesses, called from a Texas housing project to testify about a toddler who died of alcohol poisoning, could not give the time of events because none had a job and thus nobody owned a watch. A New Jersey convict suffering from AIDS, prosecuted for biting a guard to spread the disease, said it was his only way to publicize the unavailability of AIDS drugs to prison inmates. The trial of a teen-age girl from inner-city Milwaukee, who shot another young woman to death because she wanted her leather coat, revealed that guns were commonplace in the defendant's life—her parents kept loaded pistols at the dinner table.

Courtroom trials, requiring testimony under oath and no sugarcoating of unpleasant realities, have a unique capacity to inform the public about events around them, large and small.

But critics of cameras in courts complain that the television medium too often does not present trials in an instructive way. They point out that much TV news coverage is long on cover footage and sound bites and short on explanations and analysis. They say the educational promise of gavel-to-gavel coverage is not fulfilled when broadcasters concentrate on celebrity trials and murder cases.

Those complaints have some justification. Television news—especially the local variety—often focuses (along with print journalism) on the sensational. But if cameras are not allowed inside the courtroom, that raises prospects that TV news either will not cover the story at all, or may shortchange it. With cameras in court, legal stories will at least be covered generously on TV—and, hopefully, covered well. Gavel-to-gavel trial coverage was expanding across the country prior to the Simpson trial and will probably continue to grow in the long run. There is also talk in the television industry of developing Court TV-style regional court channels (Atlanta and South Florida would be early experiments), which would let people watch everyday proceedings in their local courts. Television has its shortcomings and its challenges regarding coverage of legal proceedings—but it can only fulfill the promise of cameras in courts if cameras are admitted there.

It is apparent that the public will be best served when two things happen: When the nation's judges exercise the courage and public spirit to admit cameras to the trials—and when broadcasters present the trials in a manner that responsibly informs the viewers. Then, both the judiciary and the television medium will genuinely have something to crow about.

Fred Graham is chief anchor and managing editor of Court TV.

7

Lessons from the O.J. Simpson Trial I

Jeffrey Toobin

The trial of Timothy McVeigh, in the spring of 1997, was the first event I covered principally as a television reporter. I was on the air a good deal and consequently had the novel experience of being recognized on the street. Each encounter was the same.

"I know you. What's your name?"

"Jeffrey Toobin."

"Oh, yeah, the O.J. guy."

Even though I'd been on television far more often concerning McVeigh, people still identified me as an "O.J. guy." In a small way, it reflected the Simpson saga's continuing hold on the American imagination. Every reasonable person concedes that the Oklahoma City bombing, with its toll of 168 dead, was a more important event. But it was the Simpson case that evoked the passionate and enduring reaction.

You could feel the differences in the respective courtrooms. Celebrities arrived daily at Lance Ito's domain in the Los Angeles Criminal Courts Building. Jaded though they were, these actors and anchors couldn't hide their glee at being admitted to what, at the time, seemed like the center of the universe. During Simpson's civil trial, in Santa Monica, Calif., I waited for the verdict on the ABC News broadcast platform as President Clinton delivered his State of the Union address. At ABC and every other network, there were silent prayers for the president to hurry up and get off the podium—so that we wouldn't be forced to choose which event deserved to be broadcast. As it turned out, Clinton concluded just seconds before the jury's verdict was announced. But the juxtaposition of the two events underlined how the Simpson case had become a surreal—yet genuinely important—national event. To be sure, the trial loomed large in the national consciousness because the media chose to cover it so heavily, rendering its importance, in part, a self-fulfilling prophesy. But the Simpson trial didn't just seem significant; it was.

The McVeigh trial, in Denver, was much more somber. The back three rows in Judge Richard Matsch's courtroom were reserved for the victims' families. Invariably soft-spoken and polite, they would often spend the entire day staring at McVeigh. They hated him, but they were also mystified by him. I remember most vividly just how many different families we saw in those back rows—that is, how many people were affected by the bombing of the Alfred P. Murrah building.

But why did the public respond so differently to the Simpson and McVeigh cases? Television, of course, played a role. Cameras in the courtroom gave all of America a sense that they knew the lawyers in the Simpson case, and that sense of intimacy boosted the O.J. phenomenon. But other factors played a greater role.

The first reason has to do with the nature of public response to criminal trials. Much as the public sympathizes with the victims of crime, I believe people are more fascinated by those accused of committing it. It is a compelling defendant—not a victim—that attracts great interest to a case. History, I think, bears this out. For better or worse, the public cared about Claus von Bulow, William Kennedy Smith, and (to a lesser extent) the Menendez brothers far more than the victims of their alleged crimes. Wealthy and celebrated defendants will always generate public fascination; not so seemingly bizarre or unfamiliar criminals. The conspirators in the bombing of the World Trade Center committed a major act of international terrorism. But the public never generated much interest in their case because these defendants were so very foreign; it was, it seemed, difficult even to keep their names straight.

The McVeigh case followed more closely the pattern set by the World Trade Center trial than that established by the Simpson case. McVeigh's actions—indeed, his character itself—were inexplicable even to those of us who covered the case closely. Most perplexing was his very ordinariness. He was a typical kid described by his high school yearbook as the "most talkative" in his class. Yet if McVeigh's upbringing was conventional, his crime was obscene. Consequently most Americans shut out McVeigh and pretended that he was some kind of freak. It was virtually impossible to identify with him.

With Simpson, the situation was reversed. Through television, O.J. Simpson had been in most Americans' homes for years. We thought we knew him—in a way that we could never think we knew Tim McVeigh.

When Simpson was charged, it was as if a glamorous neighbor had been accused of a crime. Of course, much of the Simpson trial was devoted to learning that the public Simpson—the personality we thought we knew—bore little relation to the private Simpson. The hidden personality of a normal or even a celebrated person is a recurrent theme of Gothic literature; the Simpson story replayed Dr. Jekyll and Mr. Hyde on a grand scale.

But the presence of a celebrated defendant alone does not explain what vaulted the Simpson case beyond other celebrity scandals, like those involving von Bulow or Kennedy Smith. What made the Simpson case a significant national event, albeit one with many bizarre and comic sidelights, was the issue of race. Ironically, this hit home for me most dramatically in Simpson's civil case, in Santa Monica, where race was, at least outwardly, less a factor.

The Simpson defense team's famously daring defense strategy, claiming that O.J. Simpson was framed for murder by a conspiracy of racist police officers, made race the constant, unavoidable issue in Judge Ito's courtroom. From the beginning of the second trial, though, it was clear that his new lawyers would have to take another tack. In part, this was because of pretrial rulings by Judge Hiroshi Fujisaki, who found the racism of Detective Mark Fuhrman to be irrelevant to the trial unless the defense could show that Fuhrman's views influenced the investigation. Simpson's lawyers failed to do so. There was also the racial makeup of the people in Fujisaki's courtroom in the Santa Monica Court House. Throughout most of the trial, there were just three black faces there: the defendant, one juror and one alternate. Not one of the lawyers in the courtroom was black.

Still, race remained at the heart of the Simpson story, even during the second trial. For the most part, though, reporters willed the issue of race out of the civil case—downplaying its significance to the point of distorting it. They did so because of the uniquely incendiary nature of race in this country. Even the most combative reporters fear being called racist. Covering Simpson's criminal trial, we had to deal with race almost every day. We constantly risked being accused of racial insensitivity. By the time of the civil case, most of us had had it with the subject and struggled to avoid it.

But, as the civil trial wound down, the central place of race in the case could not be avoided. The single black juror on the case was removed at the request of the defense when the Los Angeles district attorney's office reported to Judge Fujisaki that the juror's daughter worked as a legal secretary for the prosecutors. Then two of the black women jurors in the first case, Brenda Moran and Gina Rosborough, wrote a letter to at least two of the civil case jurors advising them to make a deal with the same agent who represented them. The civil jurors reported this inappropriate approach to the judge, who began a criminal investigation of ex-jurors Moran and Rosborough. Moran's home was searched. The upshot of this frenzied activity on the eve of the jury's decision was that two black jurors from the first case were facing possible criminal charges and the civil jury wound up including not a single black juror. It all served as a reminder of the toxic racial atmosphere surrounding the case. All of this was reported in a grudging way by me and my colleagues, with regret that the subject had come to the forefront yet again.

The civil case ended with the jury ordering Simpson to pay a total of $33.5 million, an amount he cannot possibly afford. In comments after the case, the jury gave cogent reasons for their decision. Simpson had not been a credible witness. He had denied facts that other evidence in the case established beyond doubt. The DNA evidence was compelling. It was a familiar and persuasive litany.

Almost lost in the cacophony of the day's events were the statements of the only other African American beside Simpson in the well of the courtroom on the final day of the trial. It turned out that the black alternate, a middle-aged woman, had a different view of the case from her colleagues who had deliberated. She would have ruled for the defendant. Yet the media's collective exhaustion—and fear—on the subject of race prompted us to neglect the revealing fact of the alternate's dissent. No one wanted to tell what I regard as the truth about the Simpson case—that race was always at the heart of it.

The McVeigh case presented no comparable dilemmas. In covering that story, reporters rarely acted with trepidation. One had to be careful to respect the still-grieving families, but that assignment presented far fewer difficulties than navigating the shoals of race. Even with its extraordinary death toll, the Oklahoma City bombing was an "easier" story to cover. There was, it turned out, nothing comparable to the O.J. phenomenon and even for reporters who are genetically predisposed to hunger for a big story, that turned out to be a relief.

Jeffrey Toobin, a staff writer for the New Yorker *and a legal analyst for* ABC News, *is the author of* The Run of His Life: The People v. O.J. Simpson.

8

Lessons from the O.J. Simpson Trial II

Interview with Johnnie L. Cochran Jr.

MSJ: *Did cameras in the courtroom influence the outcome of the O.J. Simpson trial?*

Johnnie Cochran: When there's a camera in the courtroom in a criminal case, generally people are on their better behavior. You'll find that a judge who is strict, no-nonsense, even sometimes ill-tempered, is nicer when there are cameras in the courtroom.

With regard to jurors, the camera in a courtroom re-emphasizes the importance of their decision.

I know many defense lawyers want to have veto power over cameras in the courtroom. They think it's going to be unfair to their client. If a lawyer legitimately believes that a camera will prohibit his client from having a fair trial, then the right thing to do would be to oppose it.

But I think there's another view. If you have a poor, indigent client that nobody seems to care about, bringing some focus, some spotlight on his plight sometimes helps very much. The prosecutor will be a little more attentive and a little less abrasive.

You make it a fair trial. You get everybody thinking in higher terms. I try to say, Let's talk about the Constitution. Let's talk about how this one individual represents all of us. If he doesn't get a fair trial, it affects everybody else. That was one of the things I tried to do in Simpson.

MSJ: *How was the reaction to the verdict shaped by cameras in the courtroom? Did it make people more likely to second-guess the jury?*

Johnnie Cochran: Well, probably so. Part of the reaction to the verdict, though, came about because of the pundits and their opinions. If you didn't watch the trial every day and you just watched it occasionally, you would think that this was a different trial, based upon their biased reporting.

We just kept our eyes on the prize. For us, it wasn't so much the cameras in the courtroom, it was the reporting of the media that led people to think we were losing. And we were winning. If you were in the courtroom, we were absolutely winning.

People knew that. And let me tell you something. If you talk to people who watched the trial every day on television, across racial lines, the majority would say this was a case of reasonable doubt.

The best example is the glove demonstration. If you relied upon a pundit who thought Simpson was guilty, that person would never accept the fact that the gloves wouldn't fit.

But if you watched it like the jurors did, this was the most rapt moment of the trial—until the verdict. And those gloves really were tight and didn't fit.

So, that's a good example of why I believe cameras were helpful. Because if you leave it to the people to describe what happened, they bring their own biases. It's much better when you see it for yourself.

MSJ: *A media circus would have been there without cameras in the courtroom?*

Johnnie Cochran: Yes, I think so. In this case, you had everything. First, it's southern California. It's this icon. It's got race, it's got celebrity.

Now, cameras probably add to it, but I think you would have still had this great amount of attention.

Americans are fascinated with trials that have this kind of interest. There would have been a proliferation of media attention just because of the facts.

MSJ: *What are the most positive things that cameras bring?*

Johnnie Cochran: I think they're educational for Americans who really want to understand how democracy works, especially the judiciary. You have a judge there who is really sworn to uphold the law, hopefully to be fair to both sides. He or she follows the law and must be impartial.

You've got rules like the Fourth Amendment. Little kids, during the Simpson case, would write letters saying, I understand now about the Fourth Amendment. I understand about being secure in my home, that the police can't just come in without articulating a reason.

I think it told us something about credibility, that police officers will lie. Not all police officers, but some will. The Fuhrman tapes are very instructive not only for Los Angeles, but for every police department in this country because it talks about a police culture. Fuhrman says, We're like God because we can do whatever we want to do.

Now, that's a pretty frightening mentality. So I think all of that was very instructive. Police labs, including the FBI lab, are not above questioning.

I think that it also put on the national agenda the issue of race in America. And sooner or later we have to come to this. This idea that there are not racial problems in America, I just phrase it this way— denial is more than a river in Egypt. And I mean that.

Those who say that race was not an important part of the Simpson case are in serious, serious, serious denial. And that's the truth. And I will never back off of that.

I'm somebody who grew up in Los Angeles in integrated schools. I'm comfortable in whatever world I'm in because of my background and my training. And I love my country.

But I'm also an African American. I understand what it means to be an African American in this society.

It's something that DuBois talks about, something called two-ness: You're black and you're an American. So you grow up with those two things. So I understand the part that race was playing in the whole thing.

The one thing this case showed us—if people take the time to look at it—is that you can see things differently, based upon how you were raised.

Many people believe that the police generally just get cats out of trees, do all these wonderful things and just keep the peace. You talk to an African American, especially in Los Angeles—every juror on that panel, or their relatives, had had an experience with the LAPD that was unpleasant.

If you grew up in Bed Sty or in South Central L.A. and you had different experiences, your perceptions are going to be different. And we need to get that at least out on the table. And we need to move toward a society where our experiences will be a lot more similar and not so different.

MSJ: *What about the reporters outside the courtroom? How important to your strategy was it to work through the media to attack the prosecution's case?*

Johnnie Cochran: When the other side is having a field day with the press, do you just defend your client or do you try to restore him to where he was before?

We couldn't restore him to where he was before, but we could defend him and he was acquitted.

You also have an obligation, when they are out there making all these statements and everybody is assuming he's guilty, to speak out. Because at that point, it could have very well been a hung jury. And if you're going to retry the case, you have got to get something out there in the media for your client. People don't always realize that.

MSJ: *Let me ask you about four different groups and your assessment of their view of cameras in the courtroom. First, what is your assessment of judges' view of cameras in the courtroom?*

Johnnie Cochran: Federal judges, by and large, are opposed to it. They're used to running their courtrooms in more of a secret proceeding.

They serve for life. They do what they want to do. They don't want cameras in there. I think cameras would be real helpful in the federal court. The judges control that court, but people need to see what goes on.

State court judges have discretion; they can allow cameras. Some of them are afraid because of the Ito experience. But over a period of time, you will probably see cameras more in civil cases than in criminal cases.

MSJ: *How do you assess jury attitudes?*

Johnnie Cochran: I think it gives the case a heightened level of importance in jurors' minds.

MSJ: *And what about lawyers' attitudes?*

Johnnie Cochran: Criminal lawyers, defense lawyers by and large, kind of have a knee-jerk reaction that they're opposed to it. I don't want to put them in the same category as federal judges, but I don't think they want people to watch what they're doing or what's happening.

And I'm not sure all of them have a real appreciation for the importance of cameras. I think that cameras would ensure their client's getting a fair trial.

But if, given a particular case, the First Amendment bumps up against the right to a fair trial, then I think the right to a fair trial has to prevail. And I would give them that veto power.

MSJ: *To segue then, to the final category, attitudes of most defendants toward cameras.*

Johnnie Cochran: I think they would naturally be, in a criminal case, opposed to it. But I think that lawyers could do a job of instructing them and using an example that this works out sometimes from the standpoint of getting people to rise to the occasion.

From the defense standpoint, I find that it's helpful to me. Every time I've had a camera, I've won.

Johnnie L. Cochran Jr., a member of the O.J. Simpson defense team and author of Journey to Justice, *is host of Cochran & Company on Court TV. Charles L. Overby, Peter Prichard and Robert W. Snyder interviewed him for* Media Studies Journal.

9

Flash and Trash

Linda Deutsch

In her remarkable book, *Headline Justice,* my beloved friend and journalistic mentor Theo Wilson wrote about covering big courtroom cases in an age before TV made high-profile trials a national sport and the O.J. Simpson trial a world-class entertainment event.

Even in the 1950s, when Theo began covering the biggest courtroom dramas of her time with the Sam Sheppard murder trial, the elements of theater were there but the public *en masse* was not. In her book, she recalls an elegant woman at a dinner party who asked her, with some revulsion, whether watching sensational trials made her feel like a voyeur. "'Why no, not at all,'" Theo said. "'Is that how you feel when you go to see Macbeth or Hamlet?'"

"It was an easy answer for me," Theo wrote, "because I always have compared big courtroom trials to great theater filled as those trials are with revelations of human weakness and folly, with violence and sorrow and humor and pity and passion, all the more fascinating because these are real people, real life."

That long-ago conversation, which I witnessed, seems dated now. There were no cameras in the courtroom then, no legal pundits offering America their spin on what everyone had just seen, no tabloid TV to transform great tragedies into theater of the absurd. Today, if there was a question of voyeurism it would have to be posed to millions of TV viewers. Theo, from her place at the New York *Daily News,* became the dean of trial reporters. She set the standard for ethical, accurate court coverage and was the greatest advocate of openness and cameras in court. But she was so disillusioned at the end of her life that she titled her chapter on the Simpson trial "Flash and Trash."

For print reporters—and particularly wire service reporters such as I—this journey into the brave new world of electronic court coverage has been life altering. Suddenly, we are visible. As the senior trial reporter in the country, I was called upon by my colleagues to cover jury selection and do pool reports when the O.J. Simpson trial judge limited the number of journalists who could be in court. Little did I realize this would mean daily TV appearances and the end of my anonymity. Everyone was watching the Simpson trial in Los Angeles, everyone recognized me and everyone, it seemed, wanted to share an opinion with me—whether it was at the supermarket, in a restaurant or on an airplane. In Hawaii, a taxi driver screeched to a halt in front of me, jumped out of his car and said, "I know you. You're from the O.J. trial."

The effect of TV was astonishing. I began to sympathize with Judge Lance Ito, whose actions in the Simpson trial were dissected daily by an assortment of Mondaymorning quarterbacks. Lawyers in the case watched my "just the facts" pool reports and sometimes quibbled with them. In a telling moment during one of my reports, attorney Robert Shapiro pre-empted me, took the microphone and said he had a complaint: "This reporter is being too objective."

I took his comment as a badge of honor.

And I continued to cling to objectivity in spite of the seemingly endless public thirst for opinions on the case. I kept reminding myself that this was not all that different from the first big trial I had covered as lead reporter for the AP: the Charles Manson murder trial in 1970. The words "media circus" and "trial of the century" were bandied about even then. But there were no cameras in court and only limited opportunities to photograph the defendants outside of court. The grainy, mostly black-and-white footage that exists today is a reminder of how far electronic coverage has come in a relatively short time.

I have always avoided references to a "circus atmosphere" at a trial because circuses are fun; trials are a grim business. But if any trial deserved that appellation it was the Manson trial. Here was the oddest assortment of misfits ever to fill a courtroom. From the defendants with "X" carved into their foreheads to the bizarre witnesses, drugged-out spectators and Manson cultists camped on the sidewalk, it was a sideshow beyond compare.

Never mind the fact that the killings of actress Sharon Tate and six others were so grotesque and shocking that the crime remains one of the most horrifying in American history.

Recently, with the courts still in the throes of post-O.J. Simpson traumatic stress disorder, I have wondered, What if the Manson trial had been televised? It's a mind-boggling thought. Imagine the nation tuning in when Manson leaped at the judge or when he told his life story outside the jury's presence (a monologue repeated verbatim in *Headline Justice*). Imagine viewers riveted to the gruesome eyewitness account of murder told by Linda Kasabian and the story of cult life recounted by Lynette "Squeaky" Fromme. Imagine a trial in which every witness was as weird as Kato Kaelin. I think the entire country would have stopped what it was doing to watch the spectacle on television, especially when the three women defendants took the stand and confessed in gruesome detail.

It is interesting to note, however, that there are groups of people who believe to this day that they did see the Manson trial on TV, and that is largely because the print coverage from reporters such as Theo Wilson was so extensive, colorful and insightful that they felt as if they were there. Theo's first rule of trial coverage was, "Take the reader into the courtroom with you." She succeeded in doing that, and maybe we learned everything we needed to know about the Manson trial from the print press.

When Theo and I went to San Francisco in 1975 to cover the Patty Hearst federal bank robbery trial, there were no cameras in court. But there were plenty of world-class journalists. Among them was the legendary Adela Rogers St. Johns, who came out of retirement to write a column on the case for the Hearst newspapers.

In the press room, where Adela was holding court, Theo and I posed the question: "They're calling this the trial of the century. What do you think about that?"

"Ridiculous!" she sniffed. "The trial of the century was the Lindbergh trial, and I was there."

Theo and I went on to cover many more "trials of the century," and we agreed that the term was silly, something used by amateurs. In truth, every trial of significance is a mirror showing us the era in which it occurs. The Manson trial was the trial of the '60s, with its drug culture and communal cults. The Pentagon Papers trial of Daniel Ellsberg was the trial that told us about the Vietnam War and the surrounding climate of world opinion. More recently, the Rodney King trials reflected racism in the ranks of the police department. And the Simpson trial, of course, focused on celebrity justice and racism in the courts.

It is notable that after the Simpson trial ended, I participated in a conference on media and the courts at which judge-turned-TV-news-anchor Catherine Crier extolled the need to make TV news, including trials, "entertaining." I was horrified. Never in my 30 years of covering trials have I entered a courtroom with the objective of creating entertainment. Social history, yes; entertainment, no. We as reporters are the witnesses to history, the eyes and ears of a public seeking information on some of the most important issues of our time. We are also the documentarians of a justice system that is evolving anew with every case that passes through it.

Yes, what happens outside the courtroom can be news, but it takes a careful eye to separate the spin from the substance. A lawyer pontificating on the courthouse steps may provide a good sound bite, but an expert witness calmly explaining the pattern of knife wounds or the trajectory of bullets will have a greater impact on the trial's outcome. Anonymously sourced reports of inflammatory information—often untrue—won't help anyone understand what's going on in court.

In *Headline Justice,* Theo explained it this way: "Countless times in my career, a prosecutor or defense attorney offered me an 'exclusive' tip, beneficial, of course, to his own side. And every time I said, 'That's great. When it comes out in court I assure you it will be my lead that day.' Usually, the exclusive never surfaced again. The lawyers and I had a great understanding: if they tried to sell and I didn't buy, well, they were just doing their job and I was doing mine. No hard feelings."

It takes discipline and professionalism to adhere to such principles, but they are the difference between good journalism and the flash and trash Theo abhorred.

Linda Deutsch is a special correspondent for the Associated Press, one of only six active writers to hold that title. She has covered most of the nation's high-profile trials in her 30 years of reporting for the AP.

10

What Gets on the Networks?

Andrew Tyndall

Over the last 10 years, network coverage of the courts has emphasized individual trials over the judiciary as an institution of government. The cases of O.J. Simpson and Timothy McVeigh, fought out in
three trials, account for this vast difference. Time will tell whether these
recent trials, with their saturation levels of coverage, represent a new
trend in network news.

The *Tyndall Report* has tracked the content of the network news
from September 1987 through August 1997, tabulating the number of
minutes devoted to news stories on the weekday nightly newscasts of
ABC, CBS and NBC.

From that database, three lists have been calculated: the top 10 trials, the top 10 judicial stories that did not involve courtroom proceedings and the top 10 most heavily covered news stories of the past decade.
The Simpson trial was such a major news event that it ranked among
that top 10, as shown in the "Top 10 News Stories" graph. Only the
Persian Gulf War received more minutes of airtime on the nightly news.

Why was the Simpson trial such a big story?

Part of the explanation lies in the nature of trial coverage. A long
trial has logistical and narrative advantages for a news operation: All
the action takes place in one room so news gathering is inexpensive; it
has a beginning, a middle and an end so the commitment of resources
is not open-ended; it has a limited cast of characters so explanations
are not too convoluted; it has winners and losers decided by a jury.
Covering a trial is like covering an election, only cheaper—without the
expense of going on the campaign trail.

The cult of celebrity was a major, and unique, factor in drawing
attention to Simpson's case. Until some other superstar is accused of so

Top 10 News Stories, 1987–1997

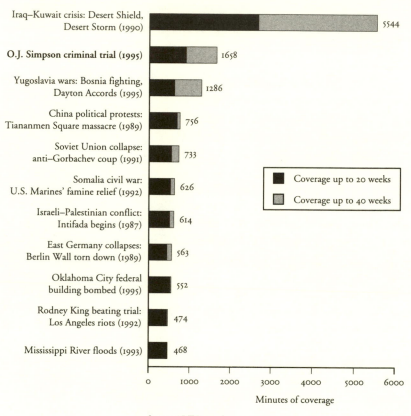

	Minutes of coverage
Iraq–Kuwait crisis: Desert Shield, Desert Storm (1990)	5544
O.J. Simpson criminal trial (1995)	1658
Yugoslavia wars: Bosnia fighting, Dayton Accords (1995)	1286
China political protests: Tiananmen Square massacre (1989)	756
Soviet Union collapse: anti–Gorbachev coup (1991)	733
Somalia civil war: U.S. Marines' famine relief (1992)	626
Israeli–Palestinian conflict: Intifada begins (1987)	614
East Germany collapses: Berlin Wall torn down (1989)	563
Oklahoma City federal building bombed (1995)	552
Rodney King beating trial: Los Angeles riots (1992)	474
Mississippi River floods (1993)	468

Coverage up to 20 weeks
Coverage up to 40 weeks

Source: ADT Research

serious a crime, it is unlikely that another courtroom will so dominate the news agenda. Nevertheless, there were other factors that teach us general lessons about network coverage of the judiciary.

First, the saturation levels of coverage of Simpson on the network nightly news reflected a fascination with the Simpson trial throughout the media, in everything from supermarket tabloids to gavel-to-gavel cable coverage to Jay Leno's "Tonight Show" monologue. Courtroom cameras, the use of which was a major innovation of the past decade, made this possible. Nevertheless, over the past 10 years, trials in camera-free courtrooms have also been heavily covered—so the importance of cameras in attracting the attention of the networks can be exaggerated.

Judicial Stories vs. Trial Stories, 1987–1997

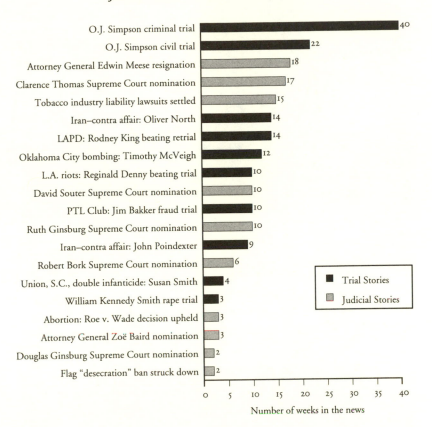

O.J. Simpson criminal trial	40
O.J. Simpson civil trial	22
Attorney General Edwin Meese resignation	18
Clarence Thomas Supreme Court nomination	17
Tobacco industry liability lawsuits settled	15
Iran–contra affair: Oliver North	14
LAPD: Rodney King beating retrial	14
Oklahoma City bombing: Timothy McVeigh	12
L.A. riots: Reginald Denny beating trial	10
David Souter Supreme Court nomination	10
PTL Club: Jim Bakker fraud trial	10
Ruth Ginsburg Supreme Court nomination	10
Iran–contra affair: John Poindexter	9
Robert Bork Supreme Court nomination	6
Union, S.C., double infanticide: Susan Smith	4
William Kennedy Smith rape trial	3
Abortion: Roe v. Wade decision upheld	3
Attorney General Zoë Baird nomination	3
Douglas Ginsburg Supreme Court nomination	2
Flag "desecration" ban struck down	2

■ Trial Stories
▨ Judicial Stories

Number of weeks in the news

Source: ADT Research

Second, the sheer length of the Simpson trial accounted for its huge totals. The responsibility for that lies with Judge Lance Ito, who lost control of his courtroom. The Simpson trial represented the American public's primary exposure to actual courtroom procedure. Marred as it was by incompetence, showboating and dawdling, the trial may have seriously damaged popular respect for the judicial system as a whole.

Third, a perusal of the top 10 trials of the last decade puts the Simpson trial in its context, as shown in the "Judicial Stories" graph. The Simpson defense, which stressed the racism, incompetence and corruption of the Los Angeles Police Department, would have been impossible without the events that preceded it: the beating of Rodney King, the acquittal of the officers involved, the inability of the police to control the

Types of Major News Stories vs. O.J. Simpson Criminal Trial
(First 40 weeks of coverage)

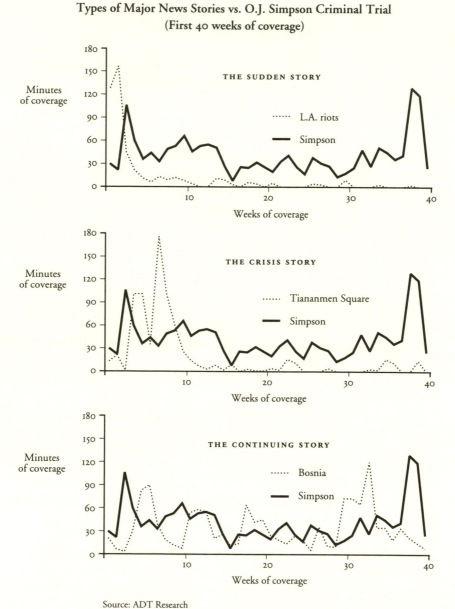

Source: ADT Research

ensuing riots in South Central L.A., the retrial of the LAPD officers and the trial in the Reginald Denny beating. Together, those stories depicted a police department that neither protected nor served the public and a court system that reached verdicts based on sociology rather than justice.

Altogether, the overarching judicial story in the United States in the past 10 years might be called L.A. Law: a crisis of confidence in the criminal justice system.

Courtroom dramas were the only stories from the judicial realm to break into the ranks of the most heavily covered stories. Apart from trials, the institution used most often by the nightly newscasts to air legal issues was the Supreme Court—usually by covering the nomination and confirmation of justices, occasionally by covering controversial Supreme Court rulings.

And the pattern of the Simpson coverage shows how the trial became such a huge presence on the networks' news agenda. Huge stories, as the "Types of Major News Stories" graph shows, can be divided into three types: sudden stories, which inspire immediate saturation coverage with a short life cycle, such as the Los Angeles riots; crisis stories, which build up gradually to a cataclysmic confrontation and then trail off rapidly, such as the demonstrations at Tiananmen Square; and continuing stories, which attract a sustained drumbeat of coverage over the long haul, such as the war in Bosnia.

The Simpson criminal trial conformed to the pattern of the continuing story. It achieved its notoriety by a sustained, day-in, day-out drumbeat of coverage. The other three big trials of the last decade—Simpson's civil trial, the Oklahoma City bombing trial of Timothy McVeigh and the Iran-contra trial of Oliver North—were all on track to amass Simpsonesque totals. They did not, however, drag on long enough to qualify.

Andrew Tyndall is the publisher of the Tyndall Report, *a weekly analysis of network broadcast news.*

11

The Camera-Shy Federal Courts

Tony Mauro

The late chief justice Warren Burger used to say that cameras would be allowed into the Supreme Court "over my dead body." Later in his life, though, Burger thought better. "I thought this might give the networks too much of a temptation," he told an interviewer in 1986. "So I just say no."

But Burger's sentiments and phraseology live on. At a budget hearing in 1996, Justice David Souter said, "I think the case is so strong that I can tell you that the day you see a camera coming into our courtroom, it's going to roll over my dead body."

Never mind that the small cameras used in many courtrooms are wall mounted. Souter was just carrying on the federal judiciary's proud tradition of stubborn resistance to the seemingly irreversible national trend toward cameras in the courts. Camera advocates have long hoped that a new generation of Supreme Court justices would arrive on the bench with less fear of the television age, but here was Souter, a man in his late 50s who had prior experience with cameras in his New Hampshire courtroom, embracing the same antique position as the white-haired Burger. No one was surprised.

It is an accepted if mysterious anomaly that the federal courts, and especially the Supreme Court, march to their own music when it comes to cameras in the court. What is routinely accepted in most state courts is still unheard of, and largely dreaded, in federal courthouses.

Trials that would have gotten extensive broadcast coverage in state courts are shielded from public view in federal courts. For example, when police officers went on trial in state court in the Rodney King case, it was aired gavel to gavel; when they went to federal court on civil rights charges, cameras were nowhere to be seen.

At the Supreme Court level, landmark cases that make headlines on everything from Internet indecency to physician-assisted suicide are heard in front of only about 300 people inside the court chamber. The American public must rely on print accounts or televised reports from the court-house steps supplemented by the work of sketch artists.

The contrast between federal and state courts is all the more puzzling because it was the Supreme Court, in the 1981 case of *Chandler v. Florida,* that allowed, if not encouraged, state courts to open their doors to cameras. The presence of cameras, Warren Burger wrote, was not inherently prejudicial to a defendant's fair trial or due process rights. And while much of the hand-wringing today about cameras concerns their effect on criminal trials, critics seem to forget that *Chandler* itself was a criminal case—the trial of Miami Beach police officers accused of committing a burglary at a restaurant.

But that decision, which ushered in the modern era of camera access, had its limits. States could experiment, the Supreme Court said in *Chandler,* but leave us out of it.

So why are cameras good enough for the state courts but not good enough for the federal courts? Why do the winds of technological change blow differently, or not at all, in the federal courts?

The long answer dates to 1946, when cameras were expressly banned from courtrooms in the federal rules of criminal procedure. In 1972, a broader ban, including civil proceedings, was written into the Code of Conduct for United States Judges.

The short answer begins with two words: Warren Burger. Long after his retirement in 1986, Burger's passionate opposition to cameras in the federal courts seems to have frozen the federal judiciary in place on the issue. Federal courts take their cue from the Supreme Court, and associate justices look to the chief justice on matters of court administration. So Burger's stance went virtually unchallenged, and the question went largely unexamined during his tenure, while debate and progress flourished at the state level.

Burger's opposition was animated by many things, but most of all by his lifelong quest for a sort of powdered-wig level of dignity and civility in the federal courts. He may have realized in *Chandler* that the Constitution gave him no choice but to say that cameras were permissible, but that didn't mean he had to like them.

Soon after he retired, I asked Burger why he was so opposed to cameras. "Television in a short snippet is simply incapable of making a proper report unless you put the whole thing on," he responded. Anticipating that answer, I was ready with a retort: How is excerpting on television different from that done in newspapers, even the *New York Times*? In a newspaper, he said, "the words aren't coming right out of the mouth of the judge or the attorney. On television, you see the person and it's coming right out of his mouth."

I puzzled over his answer at the time but have come to believe that his point was this: Television, unlike the print media, captures judges and lawyers visibly "in the act" of aiding and abetting in an unseemly, distasteful occurrence—a snipped report of a televised court proceeding. Self-respecting judges and lawyers should not have any part of television, Burger seemed to be saying.

Since Burger's departure, no one has come along to change the judiciary's stance. Burger's successor, William Rehnquist, lacks the passion Burger brought to his opposition. But he also lacks the passionate support for cameras that will be required if the federal courts are to change. At his 1986 confirmation hearing, Rehnquist said, "If I were convinced that coverage by television of the Supreme Court would not distort the way the Court works at present, I certainly would give it sympathetic consideration." Not a ringing endorsement, but at least a slight crack in the wall.

But the reasons for the federal judiciary's discomfort with cameras clearly go beyond the heartfelt opposition of a dead chief justice and the tepid opposition of a living one. It is caught up as well with the federal judiciary's vision of its place in the constitutional landscape.

Accurately or not, federal judges view themselves as apart from the rough-and-tumble disputes that are the fodder for broadcast news. They are reluctant to associate themselves with politics, especially when their decisions become campaign issues, as they did briefly in the 1996 presidential campaign.

Above all, federal judges are thankful for not having to do what most of their state counterparts have to do: stand for election or retention. A judge running for election, like any other candidate, becomes a public figure who must respond to, or pander to, the public and the news media.

"We're probably in a better position to resist the howling press than the state judges are," says Gilbert Merritt, a judge on the U.S. Court of Appeals for the 6th Circuit who presided over the Judicial Conference, the judiciary's policy-making arm, when it debated camera access several years ago.

Merritt supported camera access, especially at the appeals court level where concerns about the impact on jurors and witnesses are nonexistent because there are none. But he was not surprised, or particularly upset, when a limited, three-year experiment allowing cameras in selected civil courts ended with a vote against access.

"There's a sort of nuanced, *Federalist Papers* kind of feeling among federal judges that we're supposed to be the last bastion of independence, not responding to the majority will, and that carries over to the camera question," says Merritt. "It's not such a bad thing."

Supreme Court Justice Antonin Scalia, who has been known to walk out of an auditorium if he spies a camera waiting to record him giving a speech, once endorsed "the wisdom of the judges' ancient reluctance to engage in public debate over the rightness or wrongness of their decisions and their ancient belief that by and large, no news is good news."

This reticence is rooted not just in philosophical views about the nature of judging, but in more practical concerns as well. Federal judges, especially those on the Supreme Court, relish their anonymity and privacy. In informal discussions, many will say they think that state court judges have given up both, a high price to pay for public access to the courts through television.

The late Justice Thurgood Marshall, once counted as a firm supporter of camera access, changed his mind completely after watching Robert Bork—certainly not an ideological ally—done in, his privacy stripped away, during his televised confirmation hearings in 1987. Marshall's opposition solidified when he saw his successor Clarence Thomas, also no philosophical friend, laid bare by the Senate in 1991. Marshall told the *ABA Journal* in 1992, "After the Thomas hearings and seeing what TV did to the Senate, I said I'd not be a part of TV doing that to any court."

Justice Anthony Kennedy said in 1995, "I'm delighted I'm less famous than Judge Ito." Kennedy also said he was glad the Simpson case was televised.

Justice Byron White, now retired, spoke with rare candor in 1993 when he confessed that one reason he was glad not to have court arguments televised was, "I am very pleased to be able to walk around, and very, very seldom am I recognized. It's very selfish, I know."

White added, though, that "I suspect as time goes on the court will be made up of justices who will ask, 'What was wrong with those old guys?'" who resisted the television era.

It hasn't happened yet. As Souter's "dead body" proclamation suggests, even the new and younger justices are quickly enveloped by the Supreme Court's cult of secrecy and privacy.

The court's bleak stance of opposition hasn't stopped the media from campaigning for change from time to time.

One of the earliest efforts came in 1986, when the Mutual Broadcasting System petitioned then-Chief Justice Burger to allow a one-time experiment with live radio broadcast of Supreme Court oral arguments in the case challenging the constitutionality of the Gramm-Rudman-Hollings budget law. (The experiment would have tapped into the court's existing audio system and would have caused no disruption of the court's decorum.)

The court turned down the proposal for radio broadcasts, despite support for the proposal from justices Marshall, Brennan and Stevens. In his rejection letter to Mutual, Burger added a handwritten postscript: "When you get Cabinet meetings on the air, call me!" The comparison between public oral arguments that are already attended by press and public, and private Cabinet meetings where no press access of any kind is allowed was nonsensical, but apparently it made sense to Burger.

When Burger retired, camera advocates saw an opening in Rehnquist's less fervent views and tried, discreetly, to exploit it. Through lawyer Timothy Dyk, a former Supreme Court law clerk, a coalition of media groups in 1988 staged a quiet demonstration of how cameras in the Supreme Court might work. Two small cameras, using existing courtroom light, were secreted into the courtroom for the experiment. Only three justices attended, and their questions focused on how the justices' faces could be kept from view. The experiment failed to change any minds.

It took a nudge from Congress, which controls the judiciary's purse strings, to get the federal courts to consider the issue again. Then-Rep. Robert Kastenmeier, D-Wis., chair of the House Judiciary Committee's subcommittee on the courts, wrote to the Judicial Conference in May 1990 that "it is timely for the federal courts, at both the trial and appellate levels, to permit electronic and photographic news coverage in the courtroom."

A year later, the test was under way in civil courts at trial and appellate levels.

Actual use of the access that was allowed was spotty. Court TV, C-SPAN and a number of local television stations—especially those in Philadelphia, where a devoted local lawyer combed through the dockets and alerted news directors about upcoming cases—moved to put cameras in courtrooms. Camera access was granted to about 200 proceedings. An extensive study of the experiment by the Federal Judicial Center, the judiciary's own research arm, found little negative to say about the experience. "Overall, attitudes of judges toward electronic media coverage of civil proceedings were initially neutral and became more favorable after experience under the pilot program," the center's report concluded.

And yet, when it came time in September 1994 for the conference to decide whether to allow camera access systemwide or to drop the whole thing, the federal judiciary's contrarian nature returned to the fore and the camera effort died. It didn't help that the vote came soon after the initial media frenzy that accompanied pretrial hearings in the O.J. Simpson case.

Since then, the door has reopened only slightly. The Judicial Conference agreed to allow the 12 circuit appeals courts to decide on their own whether to open their doors to cameras. Only the 2nd and 9th Circuits have said they would.

There the issue has remained until this year. Two members of Congress, Rep. Steve Chabot, R-Ohio, and Rep. Charles Schumer, D-NY, have introduced a "Sunshine in the Courtroom Act," which would allow—but not force—federal judges at all levels to let cameras into their courtrooms. Passive as the bill might seem, its introduction was a major departure from Congress' usual reluctance to tell the judiciary how to conduct its business.

The bill, and the issue of camera access in general, has gotten an unexpected dose of support from conservative groups. Rather than wave the First Amendment banner, these organizations see camera access as a way to shed light on liberal activists on the bench. "The federal judiciary is not exempt from accountability," says Peter Flaherty of the conservative National Legal and Policy Center, which organized the latest effort, in a letter written in May 1997 to Republican leaders in Congress.

The new stirrings on the issue of camera access may advance through Congress, but probably not without a fight, public or private, from the judiciary. And if the sunshine law ultimately does pass, don't look for too many federal judges to opt for access. Federal judges don't like seeing their rulings become political footballs and won't want television cameras to make it easier. They'd rather remain mysterious.

Rehnquist himself, soon after becoming chief justice, expressed fear about the loss of "mystique and moral authority" that might result from camera exposure. "I hope," he said almost plaintively, "we don't get to the time where the members of our court are trying to get on the 6 o'clock news every night."

Tony Mauro has covered the Supreme Court for 17 years for USA Today *and Gannett News Service. He also serves on the steering committee of the Reporters Committee for Freedom of the Press.*

12

Journalism Meets Art

Katherine Krupp

On March 4, 1993, while photographers waited outside the Federal District Court in Manhattan, inside courtroom artist Christine Cornell drew the arraignment of accused World Trade Center bomber Mohammed Salameh. When she emerged, photographers swarmed to take pictures of her sketch.

Cornell depicted a bearded, anguished Salameh, dressed in white, cuffed hands clasped in front of him as if in prayer, against the backdrop of an American flag. Two expressionless lawyers flank him. The stern judge, the biggest and oldest figure, sits crowned by a medallion of an American eagle. Cornell had devised a tableau of vulnerable desperation confronted by cold authority that recalls, even more than the reality of the capture of a terrorist, traditional illustrations of Jesus before Pilate. Her poignant interpretation, which appeared on all the networks and in major newspapers including the *New York Times* and *USA Today,* gave the world a view of the biggest news event of the day.

Despite the loosening of restrictions on cameras in courtrooms, sketches remain the exclusive source of images for federal and other highly sensitive cases. Even at the criminal trial of O. J. Simpson, which was widely televised, courtroom artists captured people and actions beyond the reach of the camera.

A skillful courtroom sketch has some advantages over a photograph. Unlike a photograph, a sketch does not preserve one split-second moment, but condenses actions that take place over time. Created on site by a highly subjective intelligence, each courtroom sketch is a unique document. It absorbs physical and emotional elements beyond the reach of the stationary courtroom video lens, with its monocular perspective that flattens depth and ignores dramatic detail.

A critical look at some of the best courtroom drawings shows how television sustains old practices of pictorial storytelling. Before the widespread publication of photographs in the early 20th century, the pictorial press relied on artists' renderings. The visual language of these early pictures was similar to book illustration. Black and white sketches made for newspapers captured the basic outlines of the courtroom and likenesses of the players. The written story described the action.

Modern trial sketching grew from these popular journalistic traditions rather than from fine art. American painters and printmakers of courtroom scenes, such as George Caleb Bingham and David G. Blythe, and lesser-known illustrators of the Salem witchcraft trials and the trial of abolitionist John Brown, were not fine artists nor satirists nor muckrakers. The anecdotal realism of these popular illustrations still prevails in drawings made for television, which is now the dominant venue for courtroom sketches.

Today, most sketch reporters are trained as artists, not journalists. Some—such as Los Angeles-based David Rose and New York-based Richard Rockwell, a nephew of Norman Rockwell—started as newspaper illustrators in the 1950s. Many of the younger generation support careers as painters. They typically began by sketching a trial on their own and presenting their work to a news director at a local television station.

One of the first television courtroom artists, hired at the suggestion of David Brinkley to sketch the 1954 congressional censure of Joseph McCarthy, was eventually ejected for "behaving like a camera." Indeed, the presence of artists at work used to be considered as great a distraction as the presence of photographers. Artists were allowed to be present but were forced to create their drawings from memory. Protests against this policy, led by Ida Libby Dengrove, the grande dame of courtroom art, freed them to work on the spot. Yet artists remain, just like everyone else in the courtroom, subject to judicial restrictions. Drawings have been censored and even seized, usually to protect the anonymity of the jury, as in the last John Gotti trial.

Like other reporters, artists receive their assignments from their station's news director. They may work free-lance or have a contract with a station. When they arrive at the courthouse, they jockey for seats on a first-come basis. In cases without a jury, artists may work right in the jury box.

News directors require that trial sketches provide clear views of the major participants, no matter where the artist is seated. An artist sitting in a spot with a bad view may, for reference, glance at the sketch of a better-situated colleague. Some use binoculars to catch details. Long trials, unlike quick arraignments, provide the time for artists to compose finished drawings. They sketch out placement of figures, then, as people move around, fill in details of features and dress that do not change during the course of the day. Since the people they draw are well known, verisimilitude is essential for a good drawing. Alan Dershowitz must look like Alan Dershowitz.

Typically, only one picture—which must serve as an appropriate backdrop for a voice-over summary of the day's proceedings—will be aired. Encapsulation, then, is the artist's primary task. Nevertheless, when a singular dramatic moment occurs, an artist must try to capture it—despite the pressures of time.

The Rev. Al Sharpton's reaction to expressions of rage and fear at the Bensonhurst trial was wonderfully preserved by Marilyn Church with quick, free strokes that surround the large, striding central figure of Sharpton. The unfinished quality of the sketch, with hardly any indication of setting and details, intensifies its emotional impact.

Unlike photographs that are shot on the spot but developed in a darkroom, most courtroom drawings are created, from start to finish, before their subject's eyes. Everybody's a critic. During his hearing in the World Trade Center bombing case, Mohammed Salameh, disappointed with his image in the media, requested via his lawyer that artists "sketch him like a human being, not a terrorist." The *New York Post* responded by reproducing a photographic portrait next to one of the drawings, to support the claim that the "real thing" was actually more threatening than the drawing.

When racketeer John Gotti was on trial for crimes that ultimately sent him to jail for life, members of his entourage checked out the drawings during recess and reported back to their boss. Gotti, nicknamed the "Dapper Don" for his meticulous attention to fashion and personal grooming, would playfully wink at the artists, cup his hand to his chin or wave a "no-no" finger at his thick neck.

And Leona Helmsley once complained directly to artist Christine Cornell that she made her hair too messy and her nose too big.

When the session is over for the day, each drawing is whisked to a video camera operator, who props it up against a wall and shoots it, first in its entirety and then panning across, zooming in on the heads. This tape is shown on the air that evening, accompanied by the reporter's voice-over, exactly as videotape of the trial would be used. After a drawing is photographed by the news services or stations, which pay the artist between $150 and $300 for its use, the artist takes the picture home, and it remains his or her property.

Courtroom artists work in distinct and varied styles. New York, the art and media center of the country, home to a variety of colorful law-breakers and other engaging litigious characters, is the source of some of the most exciting drawings. The New York group uses pencils, pastels, markers and watercolors on large sheets of tinted paper mounted on stiff board for support. Working so closely together for such a long time, they have created a distinctive style based on mutual influence. West Coast artists, with even tighter deadlines to meet for the East Coast broadcasts, rely more exclusively on quicker yet less subtle markers.

The most successful courtroom drawings are not literal transcriptions of what the artist sees, nor are they imitations of the video camera's impersonal point of view. Neither of these approaches has much impact when televised. Drawings do, however, borrow from fictional dramas in film and especially television, which have been able to animate courtroom scenes effectively.

Visually static but emotionally intense small-scale human dramas, such as trials, require large facial views to convey the inner feelings of the actors. Where a film director keeps the camera in motion to underscore the tension, sometimes circling around the witness on the stand or cutting quickly from one angle to another, a courtroom artist consolidates different points of view in a single picture. For the smaller-than-life and intimate television screen, close-ups predominate. The compositions of made-for-television courtroom drawings depend on shows such as Perry Mason, soap operas and even some news shows, where the main focus is from the neck up.

An effective courtroom sketch often has a meticulous portrait of the star as the dominant foreground head, bigger in scale than the other people in the scene. Moreover, the square shape of a television screen requires concentration of action in the center. The resulting exaggeration of scale and compression of space creates an unnatural effect when the drawings are viewed in person. When televised, however, these dynamic contrasts of size and space, as well as the panning movement of the video camera, energize the drawings.

Similarly unreal, but astonishingly effective, are the vibrantly electric contrasting hues, conceived for the quivering, exaggerated light of the television screen. In another striking departure from print illustrations, flesh is deep orange with blue shading, hair is black with deep purple highlights, and clothing, settings and objects are composed of blocks and streaks of bright yellows, blues, reds, pinks and purples. When televised, these intense backdrops further animate the figures.

With these elements in mind, courtroom drawings display stylistic parallels to the work of the French Impressionists. After all, a television transmission breaks images down into tiny dots of color, just as Claude Monet did. Impressionism sought to capture scenes from everyday modern life in flickering, fleeting images. Similarly, the pursuit of verisimilitude led to exaggerations and distortions. Edgar Degas, for example, used deliberately tilted perspectives with extreme contrasts between foreground and background, as well as hot, electric colors.

A courtroom drawing is a unique hybrid, at once an aesthetic object, a social document, a television prop and a historical memento. It is a kind of dramatic re-enactment condensed into a single picture, filtered through the lens of a subjective temperament. It may lack the true-to-life immediacy of a photograph, but it conveys essential human drama that the mechanical monotony of the video camera would neutralize.

Although the reintroduction of cameras in the courts has led to premature predictions of courtroom art's obsolescence, the need for it stubbornly persists. Drawings appear on television nearly every day. Ironically, the recent televising of trials has endowed courtroom art with a greater perceived value; it is increasingly sought after by collectors. These vibrant, original pictorial documents should indeed be appreciated and preserved for those who seek a richly colored view of the dramas of American justice.

Katherine Krupp, guest curator of the exhibit "Witness for the People: Courtroom Art in the Electronic Age" at the Museum of Television and Radio, is a senior product developer at the Metropolitan Museum of Art in New York.

III

Cross-Examinations

"Coverage driven by sound bites presents several dangers. It rarely provides the public with sufficient information for an informed judgment about the outcome in an individual case, let alone the functioning of the legal system as a whole. And in extreme cases, by fomenting outrage at unpopular but legally sound decisions, it chips away at that cornerstone of our democratic system, the independence of the judiciary."
                                        —Judge Judith S. Kaye

13

The Third Branch and the Fourth Estate

Judge Judith S. Kaye

To be completely candid, I should start by disclosing that I came to the law only after I failed as a journalist. Back in the late 1950s, I saw myself as part of the "hard, tough, often cynical lot, filled with savage humor and the wisdom of the streets" that Pete Hamill describes in the spring 1997 *Media Studies Journal.*

Regrettably, no one else did. The only newspaper job I could find back then was reporting on weddings and church socials in Union City, N.J. In desperation I enrolled in law school at night, hoping that would earn me a news beat. But I quickly found my evenings far more interesting and promising than my day job. So I exchanged my press card for a pinstripe suit, and I've been in it ever since.

I tell you this not out of bitterness—things for me have turned out pretty well—but simply to underscore my own bias toward the media and therefore my double disappointment that a better job isn't done of informing the public about the courts. Not that I hold the media entirely responsible. We justice-system insiders haven't done nearly enough. Nor have the schools. But those are issues for another day and another journal. This issue relates to the media and the courts, and here's my view.

We live in a society awash in media accounts of law, feeding a seemingly insatiable public thirst for legal subjects. Pick up a paper, flick on the TV, and chances are you will find depictions—real and fictional—of the latest trial of the century, analyses of current trends in crime or punishment, reports on the doings of high-profile attorneys and a plethora of pundits commenting on all of the above.

Public interest in the courts is understandable. There is natural drama in courtroom battles, especially those that deal with life's darker or more bizarre twists. But there is more to the work of the courts than just sensational events. As the third branch of government, courts have a profound impact on how we live our lives, what rights we enjoy, what obligations we owe. Indeed, many of our nation's landmarks, which define and distinguish us as a people, are court decisions. Surely no one knows this better than a free press.

The sheer number of citizens who turn to the courts for protection of interests or vindication of claims is breathtaking. Last year, for example, the New York state courts alone received over 3 million new cases. They ran the gamut from megabucks commercial litigation to family crises, from criminal prosecutions to slip-and-fall cases to constitutional issues. It doesn't take long for what's newest in society to reach the courts, whether it's cow cloning or the line-item veto. And while other branches of government gridlock and stall, the courts forge ahead—diligently deciding the questions put to them, however difficult or controversial.

But very little of the forest of institutional competence is seen in the popularly reported accounts of the courts. The emphasis on sensational cases is one reason for this. Without question, focus on the exceptional skews perceptions of what courts do and how they do it.

I am convinced, for example, that if space aliens visited our planet and gathered all their information concerning the New York State Court of Appeals from cursory reviews of the popular press, they would probably report back to their home galaxy that the court issues five or six decisions a year, all criminal and all releasing egregiously guilty defendants to menace society.

Their report, of course, would be wrong on every count. For starters, the Court of Appeals decides about 300 cases each year, which we select from the 7,500 or so submitted to us. And most of our cases are civil, not criminal. We grant less than 2 percent of the requests for permission to appeal received from criminal defendants, thus leaving more than 98 percent of the convictions in place. In those cases heard on the merits, recent studies have shown that the court has most often ruled in favor of the prosecution. And when a conviction is reversed, rarely if ever is the defendant off the hook—the court generally orders a new trial.

Now I'm not worried about space aliens' views of our court. But I am deeply concerned about the opinions of citizens. Our democracy depends on a strong court system, and a strong court system in turn depends on public support and confidence. And if the only cases covered are a few depicted as mindlessly releasing dangerous criminals, how much respect can citizens have for the courts?

Perhaps if the selective coverage gave more of the court's reasoning, it would be less troubling. Less snappy, I know, but more accurate, more useful. Too often coverage focuses solely on the result and the personalities involved. And when superficial coverage is coupled with (indeed prompted by) court-bashing comments by elected officials, we all need to worry.

Take, for example, coverage of a recent Court of Appeals decision, which held that a felony prosecution for drug possession requires proof of the defendant's knowledge of the weight of the controlled substance. Few, if any of the scathingly critical reports bothered to mention that the court was applying an existing statute, not writing its own law for felony drug prosecutions. The statute stated both that it was a felony to "knowingly and unlawfully possess...six hundred twenty-five milligrams of a hallucinogen," and that when the term "knowingly" appears in a statute defining an offense, "it is presumed to apply to every element of the offense unless an intent to limit its application clearly appears." The legislature ultimately rewrote the statute to make clear that it didn't mean to apply "knowingly" to the weight of the drugs, but more thoughtful coverage would have identified the real problem.

The same has been true in coverage of the trial courts' bail decisions. When courts are criticized for setting low bail, rarely does the report include any mention of the statutory purpose of bail in New York state, which is not preventive detention but simply to secure the defendant's return.

Coverage driven by sound bites presents several dangers. It rarely provides the public with sufficient information for an informed judgment about the outcome in an individual case, let alone the functioning of the legal system as a whole. And in extreme cases, by fomenting outrage at unpopular but legally sound decisions, it chips away at that cornerstone of our democratic system, the independence of the judiciary.

In offering these comments, I should make clear that I am not contesting any citizen's right to criticize legal decisions or the judges who issue them. Nor am I disputing the media's right to report such criticisms—a free press is one of the great things about our system of government. But I am arguing there is a difference between thoughtful reporting and scapegoating by sound bite. And in the case of the courts, that difference matters.

In most other areas of public discourse, the remedy for unfair comment or misleading speech is simply more speech: truth ultimately outsells falsity in the free-wheeling marketplace of ideas. Unfortunately, this model has limits when the courts are concerned.

By tradition and by explicit prohibition, judges do not comment on pending matters. Sitting judges can't hold press conferences about their decisions. They must remain above the fray, preserve their impartiality and let their decisions speak for themselves. That best serves the law and all society: A decision should stand as the last word. But this means that when judges are sound bitten, they can't bite back. And since our writings are rarely reproduced in the popular press, the critical spin goes unanswered and unjust labels stick.

I still remember the acute frustration I felt listening to attacks on the Court of Appeals centering on statutory interpretation cases. In these cases, the court does its best to apply what the legislature has written. If we've gotten it wrong—or equally likely, the statute as written, in practical application, yields an unintended result—the legislature, not the court, should rewrite its own statute. That is not well understood.

The cumulative effect of this coverage is less informed and more cynical citizens, who are less likely to trust and respect their system of justice and more likely to write off the judiciary as yet another public institution that is hopelessly out of touch.

So what can be done? My plea is for more complete, more informed, more balanced coverage of courts.

More complete coverage includes broadening the focus beyond the handful of cases that involve celebrity or morbidity. More informed coverage, in many cases, may require some background in the courts and their procedures. Is that really too much to ask? Legal proceedings can be technical and complex. To tell the full story about a decision, a reporter should understand something of the interplay of statutes, precedents, evidence and arguments so the public can be told not just who, what, where and when, but also why.

More balanced coverage of the courts recognizes the limitations on judicial speech and seeks out the views of those with less access to media coverage—representatives of the local bar, for example, or academics—when legal decisions are criticized. Again, this may require legwork. But given the enormous power of the media to shape public opinion, and the tremendous role that public confidence plays in the effectiveness of the judicial branch, the extra effort is surely warranted.

A second area of concern in the media's treatment of the courts is the difficulty in getting coverage of positive achievements. Good news— or to be more precise, the absence of bad news—is all too often not considered newsworthy.

This past year, I took one small step to address the problem by changing the format of the judiciary's annual report from a snoozy tome to a jazzy tabloid. With tongue-in-cheek headlines, photographs, op-ed pieces and even a crossword puzzle, the goal was to show that there were actually good things going on in the courts that were worth reading about. We put our tabloid in jury rooms across the state and from the response we've received, it seems that people are in fact interested in reading our positive stories.

And there *are* many positive stories to be told. In every area of the work of the New York state courts, we are revisiting time-worn administrative structures and asking whether they adequately serve today's public. Through this process, we have developed a Commercial Division to provide efficient, cost-effective resolution of business disputes here in the business capital of the world. We have embarked on a state-wide effort to improve matrimonial litigation, reform the court's role in the foster care system, and change perceptions and realities about the legal profession.

We are developing drug courts to address criminal recidivism among drug-addicted nonviolent offenders. We have new Domestic Violence Parts, children's centers, automated public case information systems and even a Center for Court Innovation, which seeks to institutionalize our capacity for innovation and reform. We are continuing to revamp our jury system, reducing the burdens and increasing the productivity of this quintessentially democratic institution. I know that other state court systems have similar stories waiting to be told.

The courts in this country struggle daily to achieve the ideal of justice, often under less than ideal conditions. By and large, I believe that they do a good job of ensuring that rules and reason, not passion or privilege, determine the tens of millions of disputes brought to them each year. While far from perfect, the American courts still play a major role in making our society one of the freest and fairest in world history.

How the media portray us affects our ability to carry out our role, and it is no overstatement that the courts have not fared well in the media. Sensationalized reports on a handful of cases distort the public's understanding of their justice system. The paucity of coverage of the courts' positive accomplishments further limits our ability to maintain public trust.

The media's spotlight helps keep governmental institutions honest and efficient, and forces us all to engage in continuous critical self-examination of their work. When it comes to coverage of the courts, I think that sort of critical self-evaluation would benefit the media too.

I began this article with personal candor. I'd like to end it on that same note. There's a reason why I was so quick to accept an invitation to write for *Media Studies Journal*. Many of the points in this essay I've made before, but they have been addressed to the legal community. I welcome the chance to reach a broader audience of journalists and people who care about the media. It's time we began speaking—or, more significantly, listening—to one another. Too many important interests are at stake to do otherwise.

Judith S. Kaye is chief judge of the state of New York and chief judge of the Court of Appeals of the state of New York. She gratefully acknowledges the assistance of her counsel, Susan Knipps, in the preparation of this article.

14

Justice by the Consent of the Governed

*Interview with Judge Richard S. Arnold
and Judge Gilbert S. Merritt*

MSJ: *It seems that there is massive opposition to cameras in the courtroom, largely because of what we saw in the O.J. Simpson case. Is the criticism fair? Does it make a case against cameras in the courtroom in criminal cases, civil cases, in any cases?*

Judge Arnold: I'll be brave and start. It is certainly true, and I saw this in the Judicial Conference when we considered the issue, that the Simpson case had a big emotional impact on federal judges. It was Exhibit A for those who were arguing against the cameras.

I don't happen to agree with that view. I do not feel that the Simpson case, whatever the excesses of coverage may have been, proves that cameras in the courtroom are a bad thing. It seems to me that the coverage would have been excessive anyway.

A lot of the excesses occurred outside the courtroom, in interviews that were given, things that lawyers and other people said on the courthouse steps over which there is no control and probably can't be very effective control.

The cameras actually showing the trial were a good thing. If the trial was not handled correctly, and I hesitate to say that because I wasn't in Judge Ito's place, then the public should know that and should have a chance to form their own views on how trials could be better handled.

Maybe I'm just stubborn, but my general feeling is that the public owns the courtroom. They pay for it, it's part of their government. And the more they know about what goes on there, the better, in the long run, the courts will be. Because the public can, if it thinks that things are going wrong, form a view and express the view, and the judges can try to do better.

MSJ: *Judge Merritt, you said that you do have reservations about criminal trials, that civil trials might be more conducive to camera coverage than a criminal trial.*

Judge Merritt: I was thinking of the federal courts, thinking somewhat pragmatically. We in the federal courts, in order to have cameras in the courts serving a purpose like Richard says, have got to do two things. First, the Supreme Court has to agree to have cameras. And I definitely think that they should do that. If there's any institution that could be of educational value, it would be the Supreme Court.

It is very difficult, as a matter of principle, to argue against the right of publicity. It's very difficult, as a philosophical matter, to argue against the public's right to find out and to use the most recent technologies.

The arguments against it are much more pragmatic and less principled. But they do have some strengths. The reason the Supreme Court says they don't want cameras in the courtroom is, one, the institution is not a majoritarian institution.

It's gotten along well for 200 years, so there's an argument for history. Then there is an argument that they don't want to become celebrities, that it will change the institution if they allow cameras and become entertainers.

It will increase the need for personal security and safety.

I don't see any reason for the federal courts not to permit cameras in civil cases and see how that works out.

MSJ: *When you all were in the Judicial Conference, how much of the decision not to let cameras in the federal courts had to do with the study that showed that most of the coverage was sound-bite journalism?*

Judge Merritt: I think that is somewhat of a problem.

And that's one of the things there needs to be some standards about. Federal courts and the state courts are quite different. The state judges are much more dependent on the press because they must be elected in most states.

And so, there is more of an incentive in the state courts to accede to the wishes of the press about cameras. And that's not true so much in the federal courts, in which judges have life tenure.

I think that if we could start with civil cases and work out a way over, say, a five- or 10-year period of handling the civil cases, including the sound-bite problem, then I think the media will evolve some standards about it.

Because there is a serious problem, in a number of different respects, about witnesses and how witnesses are handled by the cameras; about jurors and the sound-bite problem, as well as others. And then, to work out some standards, I think it will be much more likely that you could apply it to the criminal cases thereafter.

MSJ: *Would either of you be more in favor of a C-SPAN-type coverage of the federal courts, which was gavel to gavel at least in the initial coverage?*

Judge Arnold: Well, it would be wonderful, if anybody could do it. There is Court TV, which, unhappily, I don't get where I live. But gavel-to-gavel coverage is a wonderful thing. I love C-SPAN; I love to watch Congress, both houses. Or the Australian Parliament, for that matter.

The most interest would be, of course, in the Supreme Court. That would be a marvelous thing for the people of this country. And people would watch that. They would love it. They would be, in my opinion, greatly impressed with the seriousness and the conscientiousness with which that court operates.

Judge Merritt: But if you're going to have federal courts experiment seriously with cameras, you're going to have to break it down to the Supreme Court level first, don't you think?

Judge Arnold: If they were willing to do it, it would be a tremendous show of leadership to the rest of the federal bench. But it's clear that they're not willing, at least the present court isn't willing to do it. It seems to me that the place to start is the courts of appeals. I suppose there's some disadvantage in that because mostly it's very dull—unless it's your case.

But the courts of appeals are places where there's the least danger that the presence of that particular medium would alter the conduct of the actors.

Judge Merritt: There's no valid reason that I can think of not to do it in the courts of appeals. Appellate judges could today vote to have their particular courts allow cameras.

MSJ: *Do you think that Chief Justice Rehnquist is in any way more open to cameras than Chief Justice Burger was? Any arguments that might sway him at all?*

Judge Merritt: I really don't know. I would doubt that he would be in favor of it. Chief Justice Burger was very much against it. I think that he [Justice Rehnquist] might talk about it a little bit more. You'll have to wait until the next chief justice, depending on who that is and what the attitude is.

I think there are some members of the Supreme Court who would be in favor of it. Their attitude is that they need a wide consensus. I think that Breyer and Stevens and maybe Ginsberg and O'Connor are willing to consider it. But Souter said it was going to be over his dead body. He's very much opposed to it.

MSJ: *Do you want to add to that?*

Judge Arnold: No.

MSJ: *If you could change anything about the way reporters cover the federal courts, what would you change?*

Judge Arnold: They need to know more about what they're doing. I wouldn't say that you have to be a lawyer. It might help, but in some ways it might get in the way.

The job of the journalist is to explain in plain English to the public a technical subject. And mostly they do a wonderful job of it. I tell my law clerks to read good newspapers for the English style. Lawyers would do well to imitate journalistic style in their brief writing because journalists communicate a lot in a few words, simply, if they do their job right.

But in order to cover a technical subject like the courts, it's very helpful if you have more than a superficial knowledge of it. And they get really elementary things wrong—a lot. They get the name of the court wrong. They get the names of the judges wrong. They get procedure totally distorted.

And I realize that the people who write the headlines are different from the people who write the articles. But the headlines are important, and the headlines are sometimes absolutely bizarre in what they pick out to highlight in a court case.

Also, I feel they don't take the time to explain the issues carefully.

We had an administrative law case in Arkansas, involving electric rates, whether or not a nuclear plant had been prudently constructed and so forth.

And this was a big thing for years, a big public issue because people are interested in what they pay for electricity. The papers covered it intensively. But they never explained *what the legal issue was* either in plain English or otherwise, never.

So the debate proceeds on a level of, Are you for high electric rates or not? There was a failure there to explain the legal issue.

Judge Merritt: I agree entirely. The coverage of courts is very poor, as a general proposition, except at one level—and that is the print press coverage of the Supreme Court in certain newspapers, where there are reporters who cover that institution as a beat.

And we could name Lyle Denniston at the *Baltimore Sun* and Linda Greenhouse at the *New York Times*. Greenhouse, I think, is wonderful. By and large the *Wall Street Journal* coverage is very good.

In order to cover an institution like the courts, you not only have to have a basic knowledge of what court it is you are covering and where it fits in the scheme of the judiciary, but you should have, like every educated citizen, some fundamental concepts about Federalism, civil liberties and how the Bill of Rights fits with the rest of the Constitution, how it got developed and the role of the federal courts as a nonmajoritarian institution.

Reporters have a hazy idea about that. Most reporters have not taken the time to develop much knowledge about that. But if they cover the courts on a regular and a routine basis, I think they would.

They've decided what the public is interested in—not what they should know about, but what they are curious about. And the court system and court processes are not among those things. What is among those things is the particular sensational case, which is still fairly well covered. But court processes, how the government works is not one of those things.

MSJ: *What the Supreme Court says is important because that is what the law is for the nation. But 99.9 percent of the federal cases that are appeals from trials go to the circuit courts of appeals.*

There are 20 to 25 full-time reporters covering the Supreme Court of the United States.

There are no reporters, or not many, covering the courts of appeals, the courts of last resort for 99.9 percent of the cases that are on appeal from federal district courts and from the Supreme Court.

What's your sense of the coverage of federal courts in that court of last resort?

Judge Merritt: I was chief judge from 1989 to 1996 and during that time we set up a system where reporters and members of the public would call in and get information about the opinions and schedules and dockets, a lot of information about the 6th Circuit Court of Appeals, which covers Tennessee, Kentucky, Ohio and Michigan.

And we disbanded that here not long ago because there was no interest. We got a public relations officer; my colleagues objected to that. But we tried out the experiment.

At the court of appeals level, we're neither fish nor fowl. We're not local and we're not national.

We're anomalous and that's fine. But we couldn't get the press interested because they're not interested in the processes of the court. Many of the cases are somewhat complex. They will cover the sensational cases independently.

MSJ: *How about coverage in the 8th Circuit? You have how many states?*

Judge Arnold: We have seven states—Arkansas, Missouri, Nebraska, Iowa, South Dakota, North Dakota and Minnesota. There's not a lot of coverage, even in St. Louis, which is our main seat of courts. There certainly is no reporter assigned to cover the Court of Appeals as such. And I don't know that there has to be.

Part of the difficulty in the coverage is that it's out-of-town news to all the papers except the ones in the city from which the case arises.

MSJ: *In other words, the reporter in St. Louis isn't interested in a case from Little Rock. And since that's the seat of the court, you're most likely going to get a reporter from the Post Dispatch or an Associated Press reporter who is basically writing on state news.*

Judge Arnold: And conversely, the reporters in Arkansas regard it as a wire service matter because everything comes out of St. Louis.

We've done some things to address that. On what we think are particularly important cases, we arranged to release the opinions simultaneously, not only in St. Louis and St. Paul, which are seats of court, but at the local federal courthouse in the city where the case originated.

We don't do that with all our cases, but with particular ones where we think there's a public interest in it.

There is another thing that we do.

There's a long-playing desegregation case in Little Rock. We have taken up the habit of having the oral arguments in Little Rock for that case, so that the public and the press can attend. And the last time we had an argument, one of the reporters came back and asked if she could borrow or be given a tape of the oral argument.

I think that's the first time I've ever been asked that question and I said yes. I later learned that I should have charged her a $15 fee, but I lent her the tape and she wrote a much better news story.

Of course, she was there at the argument and took notes.

But having that tape, being able to listen to it again, produced an excellent news story about that oral argument. So there are things that the judges can do to make themselves more available and to be helpful to the press. And I think we should do this.

MSJ: *A lot of reporters have a sense that when federal judges put on a robe, a shield drops around them; that they are insulated and isolated and not open to questions from reporters once they come off the bench.*

Judge Arnold: There is a sense in which comment is improper. I wouldn't comment on a case, for publication. Is might indicate matters such as when a decision is likely, where the argument is going to be or that sort of thing.

I wouldn't comment on the merits of the case because that's what the court's opinion is for. The opinion is the comment. But I have spoken many times, off the record, to reporters, to help them understand an opinion.

In a couple of instances I have even called a reporter in and given him the opinion a day early, under embargo, and let him read it. Then he comes back and we talk about it. So he understands what we're trying to say. I don't do that much. But I will say this: In the times that I've done it, I've never had a problem with it.

Judge Merritt: I learned a long time ago, when I was a United States attorney, that the people who were covering federal courts in Nashville could be trusted and if you didn't cooperate with them, they would get stuff mixed up.

I talk to reporters two or three times a week, on the average. I usually talk off the record. But I do not want something that I have done or something that our court has done to be misunderstood and misperceived.

MSJ: *How do your colleagues feel about that?*

Judge Merritt: Some feel similar, in the way that Richard does and I do, and others don't.

MSJ: *Recently, there have been a lot more lawyers appearing as commentators on trials. From what you've seen, how would you assess their performance?*

Judge Arnold: Some of them are very good. Some of them say things that are unbelievable. Of course, you're talking about TV. I watch TV a lot, and I yell at the TV set a lot. But I only do it at home, so no one knows exactly who it is that I'm yelling at.

But some of these pundits, the pontificators, lawyers who voice legal opinions on television are astounding. That's just a subjective reaction.

There's a fellow named Jack Ford on NBC who I think is pretty good. But some of them are unnecessarily confrontational. Some of these programs get a "defense lawyer" and a "prosecutor" together, and they yell at each other, say outrageous things. I don't think that contributes to the sum total of public good.

MSJ: *The Oklahoma City trial was widely seen, I think by many reporters, as kind of the antidote or opposite of the Simpson trial, with Judge Matsch being tougher, more restrictive. Do you think that's going to have a long-term impact on how judges handle the press in their courtroom?*

Judge Merritt: I think that is likely to have an effect. There is a much greater tendency on the part of judges today to put things under seal and to prevent the press from going about sensitive matters than there was 20 years ago.

MSJ: *Is that a positive thing?*

Judge Merritt: Bad. Bad. In general, it's bad. There are occasions where things should be put under seal, and we could discuss what those are. That's a more technical problem. But in general, the tendency is in the wrong direction—putting too much under seal and not taking into account that the judiciary is first and foremost a public institution. Our records, unless there is an exceedingly good reason, should be open to the public.

MSJ: *What about criminal trials? In the Oklahoma City case, journalists got material from the defense and then rushed to publish to try to break the story.*

Judge Arnold: It's my view that lawyers, as part of their ethical obligations, should be very careful about what they say to the press. I would say that with respect to criminal trials and in civil cases.

I personally don't like the practice of lawyers giving interviews on the courthouse steps and arguing their case to the reporters. I didn't do it, when I practiced law, and I don't think that lawyers should do it. Nor do I think that it helps their case.

I don't know why they think that it helps them win a case to have a press conference. But that is a view that is widely accepted among some lawyers today.

Judge Merritt: I agree entirely with that.

There are situations where the press transgresses what is reasonable. And I think we have to let them transgress it.

You've got the judicial institution and the press institution, it seems to me, both going astray because of the pressures of the moment.

It's not just the judicial institution that needs to have better standards and take into account the interests of the public. I think that the press needs to have better standards and take into account the interest of the system of justice in our society, in addition to just the momentary interest in getting it out to the public to beat some competition.

MSJ: *Just to go back to the McVeigh case for a moment. During that case, the Dallas Morning News, acting on a leak that it picked up from apparently a disgruntled defense lawyer, got a confession from McVeigh. The AP picked it up. The networks picked it up.*

If you're an editor in Dallas, you have access to that confession. The question is, are you going to run it six weeks before the trial? And what

*are the devices, what are the processes within the system that protect a
defendant in a high-profile case and make it possible for him to get a
fair and impartial jury?*

Judge Merritt: Well, you have devices like change of venue. I also
think that there are a number of devices that the courts have—reverse
the case; have a retrial. Those kinds of things that the courts have
developed.

I think the press, however, needs to develop some standards of its
own. I think the press could use a code of conduct. I understand the
reasons why that's a controversial subject. But most other professional
institutions do have codes of conduct which are followed for the most
part.

And if they are breached, it brings down some opprobrium. And I
think a good standard for the press would be just not to publish confessions in advance of a trial. I think that would be a good provision and
an intelligent code of conduct for the press.

But as to the story about McVeigh, I wouldn't run it.

I might run it because there's no code of ethics or professional standards in the press. And so I would be accused of being weak-kneed and
not performing properly as a journalist.

MSJ: *What about providing your readers with vital information about
a major case that you perceived your viewers and readers need to know
about. And what if you say, It's my job to tell the readers and it's the
judge's job to give them a fair trial?*

Judge Merritt: Well, then that's the current view of the press. But just
as judges shouldn't act purely in their own interest all the time, which
unfortunately I think they do, neither does the press need to act always
in its own interest.

MSJ: *But what if an editor examines the facts involved and really feels
that it's in the public interest, not his own interest? The Dallas Morning
News didn't make enough on printing that story, to make a difference.*

Judge Arnold: I think that what happened should not have happened,
but it's not the fault of the newspaper. It's the fault of the leaker.

I don't think there's any editor in the world who would have failed to
run it, nor would I have failed to run it had I been an editor.

The job of the press is to find things out. And they find out a lot of things that they shouldn't know, but the fault lies in the people who tell them those things, in my opinion.

MSJ: *We have a little judicial tension going.*

Judge Merritt: That's right. Generally, Richard and I are going to agree on most everything. But on this subject, I think that the press has got to share in the problem. They should know better than to run confessions in advance of the trial.

Judge Arnold: To me, the greatest safeguard of fairness is the conscience of the jury. I believe in juries, and I believe that they conscientiously try to decide cases based only on the evidence presented in the courtroom.

It doesn't always happen because juries, like judges and reporters, sometimes make mistakes. But most times, I don't worry about the effects of publicity on a jury. I think that they are capable of, and do in fact, most of the time, set aside whatever impressions they may have received of publicity and decide that case conscientiously.

MSJ: *What I'm really looking for here is what are the devices, what are the processes within the system that protect a defendant in a high-profile case and make it possible for him to get a fair and impartial jury?*

Judge Arnold: When the jury is selected, you generally ask them, Has anybody read or seen or heard of any publicity about the case? And usually you're amazed because so few of them know anything about it, even if it's a big deal in the press in that city.

But sometimes a number of hands will go up. And then you ask each person, Has whatever you read caused you to form an opinion about it one way or the other? And most of them say no. If they have formed an opinion, you ask them if they can set the opinion aside and decide the case based on only what occurs in the courtroom.

And most of them say yes. At that point, the court and the lawyers have to make a judgment as to whether they believe the juror can really do that. And I personally think that the judgments that courts and lawyers make on that subject are usually reliable.

And the jurors who really can't set their opinions aside usually don't get on the jury. Even if they get on, they're only one person out of 12 and that may come out in the wash, because there may be other jurors who for one reason or another have other opinions about the case.

This is one reason why juries should always have 12 people and not fewer. But that's another subject.

Judge Merritt: I'm a little more skeptical about jurors' being able to set aside views that they have picked up over several months of intensive publicity where certain things are stated as true.

MSJ: *Well, let's just say a trial judge shares your skepticism. What should he do? I mean, should he allow more intensive voir dire?*

Judge Merritt: Yeah, I think he should allow more intensive voir dire. Change of venue is another way of doing it. Sequestration is a possibility; many instructions to the jury about the seriousness of their task, in putting aside their priorities. There are lots of different things.

But I still am skeptical—if you have an intensity in the press on the issue—that the jury is going to be able to set it aside. Take the assassination of John F. Kennedy: If you had to try that case, you wouldn't ever get a jury anywhere in the United States.

If you have to try the case, you may have to put up with some massive publicity about the case that has had some effect, as a practical matter.

MSJ: *What could judges do to improve their communication with the press?*

Judge Arnold: I think most judges are less proactive in relations with the press than Gil and I would be.

I used to be a newspaper reporter. I started out with a summer job, reading proof and then writing obits and then covering city government, and so maybe that conditions my attitude. But I think the judges would do well to try to cultivate a constructive relationship with the press.

We can't control them. We can't manipulate them. But we can at least give them the tools that they can use, if they're well-disposed, to explain the subject better to the public. And I would hope that more federal judges would see that that's not improper.

Certainly it would be improper, in my opinion, for a judge to start giving extensive interviews about pending cases for the record. Some judges have done that. I disapprove of it. But I don't think it's improper to use careful means to try to help the reporters understand cases better.

Whenever there's a new reporter assigned to the federal courthouse in Little Rock, I make it a point to ask him or her to come into my chambers and sit down. And I tell them, "If there's anything you want to know, ask me." I may not be able to answer the question, and I will almost certainly answer it off the record, if I answer it at all.

If you're not willing to do that, fine. That's your choice. But I encourage them to ask me things and occasionally they do. Another thing that I do, occasionally, is to call the newspaper or the TV station when I think they've made a mistake.

And I start out by saying, "May I speak to you off the record?" Yes. Then I tell them what the mistake is. And then either they just take it for their own knowledge—this business of running a correction isn't very effective—or sometimes it doesn't work at all.

I was watching the evening TV news. A story comes on about the grant of a writ of habeas corpus. And the statement is made that a horrible murderer is now free to roam the streets of the town again.

I wrote the opinion in the case. I call the TV station and I give them my name. They have no idea who I am, which is fine. I get the reporter, I tell her who I am. And I said: "You know, it's just one thing about that story: the defendant that you're talking about isn't roaming the streets. He's in jail for life."

All we did was to say that, if the state wanted to execute him, it would have to retry the penalty phase of the case.

The reporter said, "I can see we made a technical mistake."

Judge Merritt: Judges are every bit as much involved in dealing with the press as the press is in dealing with judges. Judges, including this judge, need a lot of education, about how the press works, about how you can be objective and not be so carefully tied to your own interests and your own mindset.

Judges need to understand better that we operate only by the consent of the governed. And the press is a major part of the consent of the governed. And any judge who doesn't understand that you have got to take that into account and try to keep the press and the public somewhat educated about the processes of the court doesn't do what they ought to do. And that includes being willing, under certain circumstances, to talk to the press.

The second point that judges need to understand is that there is a deep reciprocity between the press and the federal judiciary. And that reciprocity is based on the fact that the press has got the First Amendment, and it exists only because the alien and sedition laws are unconstitutional.

The institution of the federal judiciary has life tenure. It has no term limits. All of the great benefits that we have, the privileges that we have as federal judges, are because the press understands that in the end that's good for them and good for society.

And in the absence of understanding this reciprocity, you can have all these hostilities. And some of the press is often hostile to the judges because they think the judges are against them, even though there is this clear reciprocity. And the judges are the same way.

So, just as the press needs a lot of understanding of the judicial process, perhaps even more because we are public officials, the judiciary needs to understand much better the function and the role of the press— be more communicative, understand the reciprocity that should exist between the institutions.

Judge Richard S. Arnold is chief judge of the United States Court of Appeals for the 8th Circuit. Judge Gilbert S. Merritt, of the United States Court of Appeals for the 6th Circuit, was chief judge from 1989 through 1996. Throughout their careers they have been concerned with the relationship between the news media and the administration of justice. John Seigenthaler and Robert W. Snyder interviewed them for Media Studies Journal.

15

Virgins, Vamps and the Tabloid Mentality

Interview with Linda Fairstein

MSJ: *You've been in the Manhattan district attorney's office for 25 years, and you're widely known as the head of the sex crimes unit. Has reporting on sex crimes trials changed over those 25 years?*

Linda Fairstein: A lot of women's magazines came to sex crimes issues earlier than the mainstream media—whether it's stranger rape, acquaintance rape, corroboration requirements, sexual history or DNA.

There has been some change largely in what I would call the mainstream media—in newspapers like the *New York Times,* the *Washington Post;* in newsmagazines like *Time* and *Newsweek.*

When I started doing this work in the early 1970s, the *New York Times* wouldn't even cover most rape cases.

In 1977, I tried the case of a dentist who had been molesting patients. The *Daily News* and the *New York Post* were covering it with headlines like "DDS—Dentist Desires Sex."

There were some pretty exciting legal issues where we did videotape surveillance with an undercover policewoman—all kinds of angles could have been covered by the responsible media.

Instead the *Daily News* and the *Post* were literally treating the trial as this very sexy story that was a little bit funny because it was a dentist. And the *Times'* courthouse reporter said to me, "We're not covering this case; we don't think our readers want to read about sexual assault."

And that was the prevailing attitude in the mainstream media in the 1970s—it doesn't happen to our women, our sisters.

In 1974, when the corroboration requirement was being eliminated, a *Times* editorial argued against its elimination, saying it's abhorrent that a man can be convicted of rape solely on the unsupported testimony of a woman.

So the *Times* was not exactly a leader in exposing this issue. Only much later in the 1980s did they actually begin to cover these issues.

In 1986 when Jennifer Levin was killed, it was one of the first times on page A1 that they ran this kind of crime story and used it to educate the public about the issues like underage drinking, sex, prep schools, the whole atmosphere.

It was a real breakthrough for the press. Now you read the "Metro Section" and it's better done than the tabloids, but you've still got pages that read like the tabloids in terms of what crimes are covered.

MSJ: *What are reporters getting wrong when they write about sex crimes?*

Linda Fairstein: The nature of the crime and the nature of the cases. There's very little effort at either understanding or explaining to the public the different issues in, for example, stranger rape and acquaintance rape—that more than 70 percent of people who report rapes have been sexually assaulted by someone known to them, whether or not these cases are difficult to prosecute, whether or not victims are supported by the legal and medical communities and mental health communities, what resources are available, what the likely outcome is.

A lot of the issues involved in these trials, cases and investigations have not been reported or even understood by reporters, who tend to focus on the aspects that make headlines. The overwhelming coverage that the public sees is tabloid coverage, which still tends to sensationalize and emphasize the tawdrier side of the cases.

MSJ: *Is there a racial dimension to what becomes a high-profile case?*

Linda Fairstein: Oh, I think there is sometimes a racial dimension to it. Many high-profile cases are white-on-white, as most crime is intraracial and not interracial.

But I think certainly there were a lot of claims by African Americans that the coverage of the Central Park jogger case was skewed because it was a white woman that was attacked by a gang of minority—African American and Hispanic—adolescents. If you read the *Amsterdam News* coverage of that case, it was entirely different from the mainstream media coverage. [Editor's note: The *Amsterdam News* suggested that the incident was the product of a satanic ritual, not a rape and characterized prosecutorial efforts as "the work of racially motivated prosecutors with the mentality of a lynch mob."]

MSJ: *Can you give me an example of a specific story where you saw the media explore a woman's sexual history?*

Linda Fairstein: Every one of the high-profile cases—William Kennedy Smith, Desiree Washington and Mike Tyson, the Central Park jogger. In the more recent Marv Albert case, the woman has again been made to look crazy and unstable and wild.

Early on the media tend to portray the victim as either a virgin who didn't deserve this or as a vamp who asked for it. A book called *Virgin or Vamp,* by Helen Benedict, makes points that are very true about coverage of these cases.

MSJ: *A friend of mine who's a prosecutor said there's a real challenge when there is, pardon the expression, "a shitty victim."*

Linda Fairstein: Right.

MSJ: *How do you cope with that, when you have that kind of victim who is not automatically going to get sympathy from the press?*

Linda Fairstein: Ultimately you are trying to convince the press and the jury that people with alternative lifestyles are going to be far more vulnerable than I am, going home to a doorman building.

In cities like this, we have drug addicts, prostitutes, homeless and recreational drug users. You'll get the sexually active woman who may have had intercourse with 10 people in the preceding month.

You can't change the victim. It doesn't work. What you argue instead is, you don't have to take this woman home to your dinner table and let her sleep in your extra bedroom tonight. But you do have to understand why she was vulnerable and that she's entitled to the same coverage of the law as the rest of us.

MSJ: *What do you do when one of your victims has been stigmatized as a vamp?*

Linda Fairstein: You bemoan the fact, but sometimes there's not much to do to change that impression via the media. Take a high-profile case like the Robert Chambers/Jennifer Levin case, in which I was the lead prosecutor. It was a murder case without even an element of sexual assault charged in it. But because the defense claim was rough sex, it was tried as a "sex case."

Jennifer Levin was portrayed as a bad girl. The "she asked for it" attitude that cloaked that case, even in the media, was almost impossible to come out from underneath. There were 18 months of pretrial publicity with that case before we walked into the courtroom.

MSJ: *Is the impact of the press on your cases greatest in the pretrial phase?*

Linda Fairstein: The period of greatest impact is pretrial because that could be anywhere from three months to a year. Depending on the coverage, people can become immersed in reading about the case. And from this reading-and-listening public come the people who sit on our juries. After the trial has begun, the jurors are given a rule—that they don't read or listen to media accounts of the case. Most people try hard to comply. But it's almost impossible with the highest-profile cases for it to really happen.

When a case like Chambers, the jogger, the subway bomber or the World Trade Center bomber is on trial in New York—and it is literally a page A1 headline—our jurors are coming to work on the subway and the bus. I can remember trying those cases and standing on the subway when Robert Chambers was on trial and seeing the "Rough Sex" headline in the hands of other riders. I mean, you can't sit on a train and not see what's there.

And you deal with a jury pool that is just saturated with that kind of information. You hope that you get jurors who are telling you the truth, that they can set aside what they've heard and just listen to the evidence in the courtroom. In the end, both sides use the press to great advantage before you get anywhere near the trial stage.

So there's not much you can do, and here we get into two brands of prosecution. Bob Morgenthau, whom I respect enormously, who has been DA here since '76, has a very strong position that we don't try our cases on the courtroom steps or to the press. We try them in the courtroom.

And I respect that. And yet, it can be heartbreaking to read headlines every day that don't reflect what your facts are or what you'd like the public to be hearing about a case.

You have the Gil Garcetti tactic during Simpson, which Bob Morgenthau would never stand for, of holding press conferences where his prosecutors would stand before the mikes and talk about their evidence and talk about their witnesses. We'd never do that here.

MSJ: *What's the point of the approach that you take here in New York County?*

Linda Fairstein: The more noble effort to believe that these cases should only be tried in the courtroom. That it's inappropriate for prosecutors to be spinning the case to the media. It has its roots in a more remote time and place, before the media covered sex crimes cases regularly, before cameras were anywhere near the courtroom, not to mention *in* it. We've become much more media conscious of these cases. Every large prosecutor's office has a public relations office.

We certainly do. It used to be sort of a one-person operation. It's much larger now, to respond to all the media requests that we get and the fact that we're much larger and there are many, many high-profile crimes being investigated and prosecuted in a city like this all the time.

MSJ: *If you're not trying the case on the court-house steps, what is the function of the public information officer?*

Linda Fairstein: Sometimes it is to release information at what we think are the appropriate times. When there's been an indictment and an arraignment and the indictment then becomes public record, and the 10 stations and five newspapers who report ask for those documents, that's the office that produces it.

There's basically a rule here that line assistants don't give interviews and talk to the press. Everything goes through the public information office if there's going to be a statement.

MSJ: *What's the rationale behind that?*

Linda Fairstein: There are now 600 of us here. And I don't know if it's a science, but it's certainly an art to be able to deal well with the press. Our young assistants have no experience doing it, and I think Mr. Morgenthau firmly believes that it just isn't appropriate for John Doe to tell every reporter about the facts of his case.

MSJ: *You're in the courtroom working on a case. There's another version of the case that appears on television and in print.*

Linda Fairstein: It's probably one of the most frustrating aspects of having to work on a case that's covered by the press. I'll use the Chambers case again as an example.

You've tried your guts out and you've had a good witness all morning who makes a compelling point in the prosecution's favor and puts a very important piece of evidence in play and moves your position forward.

Then you put your second witness on at 2:15 and the reporter is there for the 3 p.m. to 5 p.m. period when the witness is cross-examined and perhaps hurt on the cross-exam. On the evening news at 11:15 you see a minute-and-a-half clip of the case, with a reporter who may have been in the courtroom for an hour that day. So the lead story becomes the fact that the medical examiner was uncertain about the toxicological findings.

And you lose what you know was a successful day in court with a piece that doesn't at all go to the merits of the case. It's one piece of 16 days of medical testimony.

And yet, you know what the public is absorbing from your six hours in the courtroom: This was a bad day for the prosecution. So you have that minor frustration that you feel.

And this happened frequently during Chambers and during the jogger trial, which my colleague Elizabeth Lederer tried. We present the evidence and then at the end of the day the defense attorney, because they operate under different self-imposed rules, will stand on the courthouse steps answering a reporter's questions. And that's frustrating.

And then your lawyer friends start calling and saying, "Sorry you had such a bad day in court."

Well, I didn't have a bad day in court. Sometimes I do, but sometimes it's an entirely different package that's being presented during the two minutes of the evening news. But that's where the public is going to get its information.

MSJ: *When you're concerned about how that case looks to the world at large, is your concern somehow that the coverage bounces back onto the jurors? Or are you concerned with the way the wider public is going to view the proceeding?*

Linda Fairstein: In that particular instance, my concern is more with the general public. It is somewhat with the jury, especially the less well-educated or less-intelligent jurors who, if they are in fact watching those news events, may put aside their own thoughts for the day if Jim Jensen is telling them this is what happened in your courtroom today.

People always used to say: "Ignore what's in the tabloids; ignore what's in the newspaper. Just do your work." But every day in this office we get a package of clips that are all of the clips from every newspaper that the press office reads about anything that has to do with a case or an investigation in Manhattan.

And when you're on trial with a highprofile case, there are pages and pages of clips. And I always made it a practice to read all of those clips because one of the things I had learned was if that's the way that the reporter perceives what's happening in the courtroom, maybe that's what the jury is getting and maybe I need to call another witness to make the point I was trying to make that went over the reporter's head.

Maybe if the reporter thinks that rape victim shouldn't have had five drinks before she went to the guy's apartment, I need to be able to call five other people from the bar or the bartender to say that she was still standing, still walking.

MSJ: *What about the time of an arrest, when police officers present a suspect at a press conference, before television cameras and reporters, doing the "perpwalk." How does that affect your case?*

Linda Fairstein: Ugh, in any variety of ways. Generally not for the good at all. We've had examples in which innocent people have been exposed and the resulting investigation is that they did not commit the crime with which they've been charged. I can think of two of those cases that I prosecuted. And one of those men was a medical professional.

I don't know how you ever repair the kind of damage that's done at that point in time when there's really no crying need to do that perpwalk. And there are smaller ways they can hurt cases.

You can have cases in which defendants' photographs appear in a newspaper before your witnesses to the robbery have seen a lineup. That can compromise the actual legal proceeding of doing a lineup because they will have seen them on television being held by a cop. The defense can say that the witness did not have an independent source to make an identification, for the purpose of picking him out of a lineup.

Rather, that the witness is responding to the very strong suggestion of the police that the individual in handcuffs was the one who robbed or raped the victim.

So it can really deprive us of evidence. It can blow a case. There's no legitimate need for it to be done.

MSJ: *What do you say to journalists who go to cover something like that?*

Linda Fairstein: Nothing. I can understand them going to cover it. I'm intelligent enough to know that if you offer them that opportunity, they're going to be there covering it. That's one instance where I don't put the weight or the blame on them.

MSJ: *Has diligent and ethical reporting ever helped make a case for your office?*

Linda Fairstein: I can't think of a case in which we needed or used the media to get a conviction, or a case in which the media contributed to the prosecution's understanding or coverage. And I don't mean it as a knock.

What I do like about the press now is that reporters are, for the first time in the last 10 years, educating the public about many of the issues. There are a lot of stories in a lot of newspapers—mainstream and tabloid—about acquaintance rape and date rape. People are now talking about DNA. What's the value of DNA in a case like this? There are many more of these sort of sidebar stories that do attempt to explain the issues. And that's the only way the general public begins to get educated about it.

Although sexual assault has been written about a lot in mainstream and tabloid media, I think making people read about it is something else. A lot of people just skip over the issue if it doesn't interest them or hasn't impacted their lives.

But you'll still get, to this moment, in the tabs, the kind of Marv Albert headlines that are humorous, that talk about the teeth and the hair, the joking kind of headlines that relate to a very serious issue.

MSJ: *New York state's experiment with cameras in the courts just ended without being renewed. What's your opinion on the presence of cameras in criminal trials?*

Linda Fairstein: I'm a little bit insulated because even for all the years that New York had the experiment, rape victims were exempt from filming in coverage. So it had much less direct impact on my work.

I was quite vehemently opposed to the experiment when it was proposed and when it started. From a lot of the cases that I saw here, just as a colleague, friend and supervisor, my resistance to it evaporated. I found that in the overwhelming number of cases it did not distort the process at all. People did seem to get used to it within minutes of walking into the courtroom and getting on the stand. It was minimally invasive. In the average case it didn't bother me.

And then, two other things happened. In watching Simpson, and the astoundingly out-of-control conduct of the judge—his inability to control events in that courtroom, his seduction by members of the media—it was a remarkable way for the American public to see what goes on in the courtroom. I never would have believed that the People's case had been proved as well as it was if I hadn't seen it there. And then, for me, it was an incongruous result.

And I started to watch a lot of the Court TV proceedings from time to time, just basically because my husband, who is a civil attorney, also got hooked on it.

And what I thought was very valuable about what Court TV was doing was the nonsensational programming. They would have "docket days," for example. They'd go into a small town in Georgia and just do five days of everything that happened on the docket. Somebody would comment on why this is adjourned and why you have this hearing and why there's no jury for this proceeding.

In some of the trials they covered, the talking heads are of different value as analysts and commentators. I've seen people on there who I wouldn't let walk my dog. And I've seen a lawyer on there who has either been censured or is awaiting censure in New York who shouldn't be commenting.

And then there are some wonderful lawyers on there who I think really help inform the public about what's going on in the courts. So, I ended up thinking it's not a bad thing.

MSJ: *You don't want cameras in rape trials though?*

Linda Fairstein: I don't think we're ready, and I think until the public and the media treat rape victims better they shouldn't have to be exposed to that. It's still such a new thing that victims are getting decent attention from the courtroom. So I understand that, and as selfish as it is, I would still argue for that exception.

MSJ: *You're on an American Bar Association team that offers advice on how to deal with high-profile trials. What are some of the suggestions that you give?*

Linda Fairstein: Interestingly enough, it was put together in response to Simpson. And we've had some fascinating meetings. We meet a few times a year in Washington. And it's an interesting group—there are a few judges, state and federal; some defense attorneys; some prosecutors, state and federal.

The interesting thing for me is that almost all the calls have been from prosecutors who are trying high-profile sexual assault cases, calls I would have gotten anyway.

MSJ: *When people do call you, how often do they ask you how to deal with the press?*

Linda Fairstein: L.A., Miami, Chicago lawyers don't call me. They know what they're doing. But it's probably a part of 90 percent of the calls I get from prosecutors in other jurisdictions.

Many of them don't have the Morgenthau rule of not talking to the press, so many of them want to be spinning from the beginning.

And often there's sort of a tone of despair of like—what can I do? This is what the press has done already. This is a good guy, he's from a good family, he's clean-cut, he couldn't have done this. How do I counter that image?

MSJ: *What kinds of suggestions do you give them?*

Linda Fairstein: It starts with whether or not they can make statements and talk to the press. Often I tell them to try and find an ally in the press; somebody who is willing to do a feature about the issues or some aspect of the prosecution's side of the story.

It's finding out who you can trust in your press pool that you go off the record with. If there is an image you want to correct about what they're presenting, then obviously that's a really dangerous thing if you don't know the person. A lot of our pool is so stable, and I know who I'm dealing with.

I can say to Barbara Ross of the *Daily News,* "Hey, don't go there; I promise you, you'll see why next week." And tell her something off the record. A new guy on the block comes in and says he's from whatever newspaper—I'm not going to have that kind of conversation with him.

There are prosecutors who say, "I'm not talking to anybody." But one value is what you get from a good reporter. Our press office is around the corner on the eighth floor, maybe 50 yards from where we're sitting.

Most of them who have been around know where I am, and they will come in. Very often, from the good reporters I will get droppings that I didn't know about that might send me in a different direction, in a good direction.

There are a lot of good reporters around, and a lot of them have information. Very often they will come in looking for a tidbit from me, and they're willing to trade something for it: "Did you hear what the defense is saying about your psychiatrist expert witness? That he's been indicted in Wisconsin for child abuse?"

Well, I didn't know that, and so part of it is using the same people who are trying to use you. And there's a value to that. But a lot of these guys feel burned by reporters or don't trust the coverage if it hasn't gone their way. And I try and urge them to be a little more open-minded than that.

Linda Fairstein is chief of the Sex Crimes Prosecution Unit in the District Attorney's Office of New York County and author of the novels Final Jeopardy *and* Likely to Die. *Robert W. Snyder interviewed her for* Media Studies Journal.

16

Feeding the Ravenous Appetite of the Press

Interview with Barry Scheck

MSJ: *Most reporters would say that by searching out the facts of a case and being the eyes and ears of the public, they help ensure a fair trial. As a law professor and a defense attorney, does it look that way to you?*

Barry Scheck: I have no quarrel with the reporter trying to find out everything that he or she can about a case and reporting it accurately, trying to find out whether a defendant is guilty or innocent or to make a vigorous inquiry into any aspect of a case.

However, the perennial tension that lies at the heart of the fair trial/free press controversy concerns the desire of people in the press to know privileged information that should not be disclosed if you're going to have a fair trial.

I'm talking here not just about information that is privileged because it is the statement of the defendant or it's part of the confidential information of the defense camp, but also information that is secret and privileged from the point of view of the prosecution, and certainly, the privileged decision-making process of the courts themselves.

When you disclose this kind of information prior to the trial, and the information comes out in a fashion that is not orderly and not within the trial process itself, you will skew the process and make it unfair.

And from the point of view, not just of the defense but of the prosecution and the court, what we see now in high-profile cases is a ravenous appetite on the part of the press to obtain information that they have no legal right to get. And when they get it and disclose it, it undermines the fairness of our trial processes.

No better example exists than the disclosure of information prior to the selection of the jury in the Oklahoma City bombing case, the trial of Timothy McVeigh.

McVeigh's lawyers are saying, as I've seen them quoted in the press, that the reporter for the *Dallas Morning News* obtained from a computer thousands of files on the case that contained privileged information, conversations between McVeigh and his lawyers; reports by defense investigators; reports from the prosecution itself that they were obligated by discovery to turn over. But they're not public documents.

It may be from the point of view of the reporter a great story. But it seems to me, if you think that that's such a great story—to get this information in advance, before it's revealed in court in the natural and orderly processes of a trial—fine, print it. That's your First Amendment right once you get it.

But it's also the obligation of government to put you in jail because, as far as I'm concerned, that's theft. It's the kind of thing that we ordinarily overlook in the way the news is obtained from other governmental sources because leaking is part of the business of government and it's part of the business of the press.

I'm not saying that there's necessarily going to be a prior restraint, but I think that if you think that's such a great story, then you ought to be willing to go to jail if that's the means by which you got it. That's the distinction that's been overlooked. And I'm really curious to see what, if anything, is done, subsequent to the McVeigh case, about what was reported to be these kinds of wholesale leaks.

MSJ: *Do you think some of the gag orders around the McVeigh case in Denver, some of the restrictions on what you can do, were onerous?*

Barry Scheck: There was a big untold story about the McVeigh case.

Judge Matsch did a number of things, which I think everybody agrees were very good. For example, he allowed the lawyers to talk until the eve of jury selection. Then he gagged them. That seemed reasonable, pursuant to Rule 3.6 and the *Gentile* case and the nature of that proceeding [3.6 is a section of the American Bar Association's rules for the lawyers' conduct; in the *Gentile* case, the U.S. Supreme Court set limits on what a lawyer could say to the press]. And I was not particularly bothered by the wall he put up so that journalists couldn't see the jurors.

But I didn't think enough attention was paid to the extraordinary restrictions that he imposed upon arguments. Most of the important legal motions in the McVeigh cases were argued in camera [in private, or in a judge's chambers], early in the morning, under seal.

Some of these restrictions one can understand to the extent that Judge Matsch was trying to prevent disclosures that could poison the jury pool for purposes of the upcoming Nichols case.

But it did seem to me that some of these restrictions probably couldn't be justified on those grounds and were part of his well-known views that were somewhat antagonistic to legal commentators and extensive press coverage.

MSJ: *Why do you think the press missed this?*

Barry Scheck: Lawyers for the press did appeal these restrictions, but when the appellate courts literally sat on those appeals, the press stopped complaining.

They began to accept it, primarily because they suddenly seized upon this trial as the anti-Simpson example. And I was troubled by that. I thought that was a failure of good journalism. They sort of picked the angle that they decided to have in that story and anything Judge Matsch (for whom, incidentally, I have a tremendous amount of respect) did was going to be right.

They just began to take what the court was offering, without a full understanding of all the secret rulings that were truly dictating the kind of proceeding that they were seeing.

MSJ: *In your experience, are the police and the prosecution more likely to leak to reporters?*

Barry Scheck: Everybody leaks, to the extent that they see that it is going to be to their advantage. In that respect, criminal trials are supposedly no different than any other kind of political event or news event that reporters commonly cover.

In fact, right now, the rules of professional responsibility recognize this reality. Criminal defense lawyers are now allowed to make statements to level the playing field if law enforcement officials issue prejudicial leaks at the beginning of a criminal investigation. But you are limited in your response to clearing up the prejudicial publicity.

MSJ: *Writing in* Media Studies Journal *a few years back, William Kunstler said: "The responsibility for seeking and finding press outlets for defendants with 'newsworthy' cases falls squarely on the shoulders of their defense counsel. Whenever and wherever practicable, fire must be met with fire, and it is often only lawyers who have any chance of igniting a flame friendly to their clients." Do you work that way?*

Barry Scheck: Yeah. I'll give you a pretty simple example. Here [at Cardozo Law School of Yeshiva University] we are involved in this work at the Innocence Project.

We're using DNA technology to overturn these wrongful convictions, and the impact that these cases have had upon the criminal justice system in the various different jurisdictions has been absolutely enormous.

When you get involved in a high-profile case, it's your responsibility to try to use it to good ends. I made a deal with NBC that they would do four shows on "Dateline" about cases of individuals that have been falsely accused and wrongly convicted—as it turns out, not any case that I was working on as counsel. And that we would also take those four shows, and in the terms of the trade, we'd repurpose them for a cable show on MSNBC where we were able to deal with the issue in some greater depth.

They readily agreed to that deal, and it's been a win/win situation for everybody because the stories that they're looking at are all good stories that they probably would have covered anyhow.

It's just that I was in a position to bring those stories to their attention, and they applied ordinary journalistic standards, standards that I take very seriously about all these kinds of cases.

MSJ: *Do you think that most reporters who write about DNA evidence understand it enough to adequately assess the strategy that you used, the way you interpret DNA?*

Barry Scheck: No. It is always remarkable to me, with the tremendous resources available to the press, that most reporters don't really go out and attempt to educate themselves seriously about DNA testing. And there are always oversimplifications of what it means to the criminal justice system.

In the Innocence Project at Cardozo, we have assisted or represented 34 individuals who have been able to demonstrate that they were wrongly convicted of a crime, through the use of DNA evidence.

And overall, there are now 45 such individuals in this country. Many of them death-penalty cases. We're using DNA evidence on the old samples. We will always have the tests replicated by prosecution laboratories. We do everything we can to ensure that there is no contamination of samples, that the testing is done correctly, in accordance with the highest scientific standards.

So Peter Neufeld and I have always viewed our work in this area as a matter of law reform to move forensic science, and the use of DNA testing in particular in forensic science, forward—for law enforcement, for defendants, for the sake of the system as a whole. And since the Simpson case, we were able to pass model legislation in the state of New York and set up what's known as a forensic science review board, which regulates all the crime laboratories in the state of New York, including the DNA laboratories.

Peter and I have been appointed by the chief judge of the New York Court of Appeals and the speaker of the assembly to serve on that commission, and we have for the last two years. And we're doing a lot to create DNA data banks, making sure all the laboratories in New York state area are accredited.

Oddly enough, the Simpson case actually helped in this effort, because whether people believed O.J. Simpson was guilty or innocent, the entire forensic community, I believe, has recognized that the conduct of the Los Angeles Police Department Crime Lab, their DNA laboratories and the Medical Examiner's Office was deplorable. It's not the way to handle a major case.

And as a consequence, laboratories all across the country have been seeking accreditation and seeking to reform their practices. As for the Simpson case, that's the only silver lining I've ever seen in it—it has really helped advance the cause of raising the standards of forensic science. And we think we've been a part of that, and we'll continue to be.

MSJ: *Part of the Simpson case that got a lot of notoriety during the criminal trial was the use of cameras in the courts. How do you think the presence of cameras affects the trial?*

Barry Scheck: I can think of a lot of good aspects to the way behavior is sometimes changed by cameras in the courtroom. Sometimes judges and lawyers on either side strive to be on their very best behavior. Similarly, there are benefits that occur when witnesses are seen on television and people call in with facts about the case.

On the other hand, television has this feedback effect that influences the behavior of participants in a very negative way. I saw a lot of that, frankly, in the Simpson case and in other trials.

Judges take a lot of heat with viewers second-guessing their decisions every day. And the lawyers, in terms of their demeanor, and everything they do, are subject to a different kind of criticism when the trial is televised than when it isn't. It does affect their behavior.

And when you get into a situation like Simpson, where all of a sudden the tab-loidization of the trial begins to occur and everything devolves to the lowest common denominator in terms of coverage, it gets really hard to handle. But even more important than that, I think it profoundly affects witnesses. We saw it in the William Kennedy Smith case, for example, where all of a sudden, the tabloids began paying witnesses $25,000, $50,000 for their testimony, which fatally undermines the witness.

If you had C-SPAN-type coverage, where people see it every day, it would be much better. And if the coverage were better, then the experiment of cameras in the courtroom, I think, would work out better.

I'd love to see the franchise on televising trials in a particular jurisdiction bid upon by public interest entities. The C-SPAN-type court channel would get the first day of coverage. You would be able to see the trial from beginning to end.

Then, if you gave that particular channel the exclusive right to broadcast the pictures for that day and the regular news could get it a day later, I think that would be an interesting experiment. Because then at least the public would be drawn to the best and least-editorialized version of the events of the trial.

You wouldn't be totally restricting the press from having access to the witnesses' testimony, but there would at least be one good shot in terms of having people focus on the full events of the trial that day.

MSJ: *A lot of the pieces that I've read about you mention your roots in the '60s and all the work that you did in legal aid law. In the '90s, are reporters less likely to respect those characteristics than they were, say, 30 years ago?*

Barry Scheck: It's very peculiar. Basically, I've been either a public defender or a law professor for my entire career, representing almost predominantly the indigent. I work with DNA and the Innocence Project and virtually all the work we've done has been pro bono work.

But the O.J. Simpson case sort of skewed everything. People had their responses to that and nothing is going to alter them. And I don't think that the coverage was particularly sophisticated in that regard.

It was very odd to me that people wouldn't even focus on the fact that our clinic had represented Hedda Nussbaum and a lot of battered women before it was fashionable to take up the cause of battered women.

So there's not a lot of room for nuance when you get involved in these kinds of cases, and one learns that the hard way. But it goes with the territory, I suppose. Of course, I had no idea what the Simpson case would eventually become.

I suppose we could have dropped out of it, although that presents certain duty-of-loyalty problems. Once we saw how absolutely enormous it was going to become, we had obligations as lawyers and we went through with them. I don't regret it for a second.

MSJ: *From your perspective, do reporters tend to favor either the prosecution or the defense?*

Barry Scheck: I don't think that there's any typical bias one way or the other. What reporters are generally interested in is a good story. And the more they tend towards writing for tabloid publications, they're interested in the best tabloid story.

They like people that are good copy. That give them good stories. It tends to be, however, that there are more law enforcement sources from which to get information. In a criminal case, what ordinarily happens is that the initial rush of publicity is always in favor of the prosecution. After all, there's an arrest, there's the crime, and the defense is literally on the defensive in most instances.

MSJ: *Are there particular reporters whose work you admire that you think is worth emulating in their coverage of the courts?*

Barry Scheck: Sure. I've always thought that lawyers generally owe a debt of gratitude to Steve Brill. I think that *American Lawyer* magazine and the in-depth coverage it gave to all kinds of issues involved in the practice of law, and the kind of coverage that you could expect from those journalists was always a cut above everyone else.

I should say, by way of disclosure, that Steve and I went to college together and we're friends for a long time.

MSJ: *You've said that there should be a code of ethics for lawyers who serve as commentators in the news media.*

Barry Scheck: Lawyers bear a lot of responsibility for the nature of coverage and commentary when we're called upon as experts by the media to talk about what's going on in legal cases. And some of these aspirational standards may sound almost silly but they're pretty simple.

For example, it's the job of a commentator to be informed, to be prepared. What's happened to many lawyers is that, during the course of the Simpson case and thereafter, for example, the local news show producers would call them in and say, Hey, here's your gig: Tell us what you think of what happened today.

And they would not have read the transcripts. They would not have been following the case on a day-to-day basis. They were earning a living. No problem with that. But they really weren't informed, and therefore they would be confining their comments to style points and spin and things that they thought they could comment on.

Much of my critique here, incidentally, is very similar to what James Fallows has written in *Breaking the News* about political commentary.

Another standard would be to disclose conflicts of interest. A lot of commentators on the air have entangling conflicts. Some may be disabling, but those should be disclosed.

We, as a profession, have to resist those people in the media that want us to come on when we don't know what we're talking about, or ask us for glib opinions that we shouldn't be giving. To be gratuitously critical or gratuitously knowledgeable, or pretend to be knowledgeable, is really dangerous.

And I think that it's bad journalism, but even more importantly, it's ethically questionable for a lawyer to do that. After all, you're being brought on as an expert who's giving some additional insight to the public, and it's a lawyer's responsibility to know what he or she is talking about.

You shouldn't be pigeonholed. You shouldn't create conflict where there isn't any. Very often people call you up and say, We will only put you on if you'll say X viewpoint, because that's what they say is good television or good journalism.

Say no. Or go on and say what you think. We have a certain responsibility to try to raise the level of commentary about the courts. And in turn, maybe we will have some effect on news producers and the powers that be in the medium to raise their standards as well.

Barry Scheck, defense attorney and law professor, was a member of the O.J. Simpson defense team. Through the Innocence Project at Cardozo Law School, Yeshiva University, he uses DNA evidence to assist and represent clients who can demonstrate that they were wrongly convicted. Robert W. Snyder interviewed him for Media Studies Journal.

17

The Role of the Media in Exposing Crimes Against Humanity

Judge Richard J. Goldstone

Too frequently there is a lack of appreciation that the journalistic standard is not that of a prosecutor and, in turn, not that of a criminal court. If journalists spent the time necessary to indict a suspected criminal, the news would be stale and, no doubt, their stories would be scooped by other less zealous reporters. A prosecutor, on the other hand, has a different threshold. It would be quite unprofessional and irresponsible for a prosecutor to indict a suspected war criminal unless there is sufficient admissible and available evidence to constitute a *prima facie* case of guilt. That victims may know the identity of the perpetrator and that journalists have the proof to their satisfaction is one thing—to be able to produce the evidence in court is another.

I have met relatively few journalists who understand that making war is not a war crime and is no ground for indictment. The laws of war only come into play once the war has commenced. At Nuremberg, the tribunal was specifically given a special jurisdiction to charge crimes against peace. The U.N. War Crimes Tribunals have no such jurisdiction. The laws of war relate only to the manner in which wars are fought—whether civilians or prisoners of war.

Humanitarian law is not an everyday subject. It is not easily accessible to the general public. I spent substantial time explaining it informally to journalists from many countries. I spent even more time explaining it to audiences—face to face or by means of radio and television. I have come across few journalists who have a sufficient appreciation and working knowledge of the subject.

One of the problems frequently faced by prosecutors is the reluctance and even the refusal of journalists to give evidence themselves or in any way to compromise sources. In many countries and in many situations, the media has come under attack in consequence. I have strong views in support of the media reluctance in that area. The first priority of the media must be to protect its own existence and its own efficiency—that, indeed, is in the public interest. If sources were not protected, then investigative journalism would be seriously compromised.

Similar considerations apply to the production of unaired TV footage. If it was widely perceived that TV cameramen and camerawomen were collecting evidence for a future prosecution, their lives would become even more dangerous. They would become the first targets in any war zone. I have no doubt that the decision whether to cooperate with a prosecutor in those circumstances must be that of the journalist concerned.

One striking illustration of the difficulty occurred when I was appointed in 1991 to inquire into the shooting by members of the South African police into a crowd of 50,000 demonstrators near Johannesburg at a black township called Sebokeng. Many people were killed and injured. After an exhaustive inquiry, I reported in strong terms to the then-South African government that the shooting had been quite unwarranted and amounted to manslaughter, if not murder. That inquiry was materially assisted by a videotape of the actual shooting, which was delivered anonymously to my chambers. I also have no doubt that the persons concerned came to the conclusion that the interests of justice in that case outweighed the benefits of withholding the evidence. At the same time, the television crew did not wish to embarrass or compromise their employer.

I have consistently refused to compel any journalist to act contrary to the interests to which I have just referred. Indeed, I would strongly support national laws to protect the privilege of journalists in appropriate circumstances. This is an issue which goes to the heart of press freedom and the ability of the media to protect the society in which it operates.

As you will know, some leading journalists have given evidence before both U.N. tribunals. None of them did so under pressure. The decision to testify was theirs alone. I am happy to say that in no case have I heard or read criticism of those journalists. This supports their judgment that they were not compromising their profession by testifying in the circumstances in which they did so. They did not compromise any sources. For the most part, they gave evidence concerning what they saw with their own eyes and not what they had been told by others.

I must emphasize that both in South Africa and in The Hague, journalists have been willing to advise and point to possible sources of information. They have done so in the knowledge that I would not compromise them. It works both ways. I have seldom been let down by journalists in whom I had confided or given background briefings in confidence. In the few cases in which such a confidence was breached, little harm resulted because the information published was correct. In those cases, such ill-advised breaches of confidence were more to the unfair prejudice of their colleagues than to my own.

Unfortunately, too many abuses of human rights are committed in too many countries. The international community has become used to reading and hearing about these kinds of violations on a weekly if not daily basis. The annual reports of Amnesty International and Human Rights Watch are testimony to this phenomenon. Yet the scale and intensity of the propaganda and hate will usually be a good indicator of what is likely to come.

In my own country, apartheid would not have lasted as long as it did if black South Africans had not been demonized—if whites had not been induced by insidious propaganda to believe that there was a total black and communist onslaught. And the degree of press control, and, more importantly, control of the only television station, certainly fell within the parameters to which I am referring.

I would suggest that what is needed today is a special "Genocide Watch" designed to call attention to situations in which there is real cause for alarm. If this is done in a responsible manner with credible and trusted people involved, it could make a difference which might save literally millions of lives. It must be done in a wholly apolitical manner and it must be based on facts that can be demonstrated to be correct. Preferably such a "Watch" should be an international organization with a wide geographic and political spread. The involvement, if not the leadership, of journalists would be essential. It must necessarily be nongovernmental, and the most well informed nongovernmental resources are undoubtedly in the hands and under the control of the media.

In the same vein and for the same reasons I would renew the call I have so frequently made for the international community to speed the establishment of a permanent International Criminal Court. If one was in existence in 1994, the terrible events which occurred in Rwanda may have been checked, and certainly the perpetrators of the genocide could have speedily been brought to justice. Had that occurred, a terrible refugee crisis may have been averted wholly or in part.

In my opinion the media is an integral and natural part of any and every human rights movement. Indeed, it is the profession most in need of protection. The first victim of any totalitarian regime is freedom of expression. No mass victimizer can allow his victims to know what is coming and with globalization of the international community, no mass victimizer can afford the international community to know what is coming. When the facts emerge it is usually too late.

If the free journalists of the world unite they together with human rights and humanitarian workers and organizations can make a difference.

Judge Richard J. Goldstone of the Constitutional Court of South Africa, is former chief prosecutor for the International War Crimes Tribunals for the former Yugoslavia and Rwanda. His essay is adapted from a speech delivered at the University of California at Berkeley on April 10, 1997.

IV

Review Essay

18

Cast a Cautious Eye on the Supreme Court

Randall Kennedy

Gideon's Trumpet.
Anthony Lewis, New York: Random House, 1964.

Simple Justice: The History of Brown v. Board of Education
and Black America's Struggle for Equality.
Richard Kluger, New York: Knopf, 1976.

The Brethren: Inside the Supreme Court.
Bob Woodward and Scott Armstrong, New York:
Simon and Schuster, 1979.

Strange Justice: The Selling of Clarence Thomas.
Jane Mayer and Jill Abramson, Boston: Houghton Mifflin Co., 1994.

In the April 1996 issue of the *Yale Law Journal,* Linda Greenhouse reveals, in "Telling the Court's Story: Justice and Journalism at the Supreme Court," that for a while in 1994, in every story involving a federal judge, the *New York Times* identified the president who appointed the judge. Greenhouse, the *Times'* Supreme Court correspondent, objected. This policy, she argued, "placed the *Times* in the position of insinuating that all federal judges are simply carrying out the agendas of their political sponsors...that they are acting as politicians and not as judges." To her relief, the paper discontinued the policy.

In her view, however, that it existed even temporarily "tells us something disquieting about the legacy of the confirmation battles of the Reagan and Bush years": the prevalence of the assumption that some of the justices are "just politicians in robes" and the prospect that "cynical adversarial or sensationalistic reporting" of the sort common in electoral politics will become widespread in coverage of the Court, thereby undermining public confidence in it.

The *Times'* policy, its demise and Greenhouse's response reflect and illuminate a deep and unresolved tension that tugs at many observers of the Court. The distinguished political scientist Robert Dahl described it 40 years ago when he noted that "Americans are not quite willing to accept the fact that [the Court] is a political institution and not quite capable of denying it; so that frequently we take both positions at once." This conflicted response, which sometimes borders on schizophrenia, has given rise to two distinct journalistic traditions.

One is the tradition to which Greenhouse gives voice. It tends to be deeply deferential to judges, views the Court as the natural haven for unpopular minorities and expresses the belief that there is and ought to be a wide separation of "politics" from "law." This tradition also implicitly maintains that it is the journalist's duty not only to report what courts do but also to inculcate within the public respect for the judiciary. A second tradition assumes no special deference to judges but assesses them in the same skeptical light as other policy-makers.

These two traditions display themselves in books about the Court that have been written by journalists over the last 30 years. For the purpose of examining the underlying premises of these traditions, books are a better source than daily news clippings because in books journalists have the luxuries of more space and time and editorial autonomy. Ordinary reporting gives the public a first draft of the journalist's observations. A book, by contrast, presents a more thoroughly considered second or third or even fourth draft. Moreover, the deeply held beliefs of journalists live on longer in their books than in their daily stories. Indeed, certain books, such as some of the ones discussed in this essay, have introduced generations of reporters to the Court, subtly influencing for decades coverage of the nation's third branch of government.

An exemplary book in the deferential, celebratory tradition— *Gideon's Trumpet,* by *New York Times* columnist Anthony Lewis—tells the story of *Gideon v. Wainwright,* a case decided in 1963. In it, the Court held that the federal Constitution requires states to provide counsel free of charge to any indigent defendant charged with committing a felony. The case—brought to the Supreme Court by an unlettered, small-time, repeat offender who initially sought Supreme Court review without the assistance of any attorney—was remarkable for the very fact that it attracted the justices' attention. After all, thousands of litigants, including many who pay large fees to specialized appellate counsel, fail to elicit the interest of the necessary four justices to have their cases placed on the Supreme Court docket.

Gideon's claim required the Court to reconsider the validity of one of its relatively young precedents, *Betts v. Brady*. The Court reversed *Betts v. Brady*, adopted Gideon's position and ordered that he be tried anew. Gideon, who had been convicted and sentenced without the aid of an attorney, was acquitted upon his retrial with the assistance of counsel.

The rendition of this story in *Gideon's Trumpet* is, in many respects, admirable—as might be expected of an author who won a Pulitzer for his reporting on the Supreme Court and went on to teach law at Harvard and Columbia. Lewis conveys in an accessible but expert fashion a large amount of basic information about the Court's procedures, customs and statutory and constitutional underpinnings. His narrative is compellingly vivid without a shred of sensationalism: A fact is truly a fact and a statement with quotation marks actually means that someone said exactly what is quoted. *Gideon's Trumpet* is careful, instructive and, dare I say it, judicious. For good reason it has been a staple on book lists suggested to students in both schools of law and schools of journalism.

Despite its many virtues, however, *Gideon's Trumpet* is undermined by significant weaknesses. Most importantly, it portrays the Court misleadingly as a heroic institution that characteristically protects social outcasts, even against strong and widespread political opposition. Lewis' Supreme Court "often provides a forum for those—the despised and rejected—who have no effective voice in the legislative chamber." This conception of the Court is widespread and propagated continuously by journalists, scholars and the justices themselves.

Yet this view exaggerates the extent to which the Court—even the Warren Court (which was itself somewhat atypical)—leads or defies public opinion. Consider *Gideon* itself. True, the Court created a new federal requirement that Congress might not have offered in legislation. But when the Court decided *Gideon*, 37 states had already provided counsel as a matter of right to indigents charged with felonies. Thus, despite Lewis' reference to "the despised...who have no effective voice in the legislative chambers," by the time *Gideon* was decided, most state legislatures already required the provision of counsel to indigents charged with felonies. In *Gideon*, the Court did not act alone to impose a novel or pervasively unpopular principle. Rather, in the words of Michael J. Klarman, a law professor at the University of

Virginia, it was a case of the justices' "seizing upon a dominant national consensus and imposing it on resisting local outliers."

According to Lewis, the racial situation in the 1950s and early '60s was "an even more telling example of the Court's function as a forum for those without a political voice." He refers, of course, to *Brown v. Board of Education,* the Court decision that prohibited states from purposefully separating public school students according to race. No case has won the Court more praise than Brown. No case has contributed more to its image as a tribunal that is above politics. No case has more burnished the myth of a heroic Court that leads rather than follows strong public opinion.

To be sure, *Brown v. Board of Education* does represent a "watershed" event in American history; it helped tremendously to stigmatize and outlaw state-enforced racial segregation. But the standard claim that Brown "started" the process of undoing legally enforced racism suggests how even well-informed Court watchers succumb to a tendency to exalt unduly the justices' handiwork (at least that with which they agree).

Blacks, of course, had resisted white supremacy for over three centuries prior to *Brown.* This obvious though oft-neglected point is marvelously highlighted in Richard Kluger's *Simple Justice,* a history of *Brown* that is, in my view, one of the very best books ever written on a single Supreme Court decision. Kluger, an editor turned Pulitzer Prize-winning author, presents an exquisitely detailed analysis of the Supreme Court's decision. But the bulk of his work is devoted, appropriately, to describing and explaining the actions of those who made possible the justices' ruling—including the local black leaders and litigants who, in the face of frightening intimidation, demanded the invalidation of Jim Crow pigmentocracy. One of these heretofore neglected figures was Joseph Albert DeLaine, minister and teacher in Clarendon County, S.C., whose extraordinary courage and perseverance nurtured one of the lawsuits ultimately decided by *Brown.* Kluger pays tribute to DeLaine in a chapter that is a model of stirring expository writing:

> Before it was over, they fired him from the little schoolhouse at which he had taught devotedly for ten years. And they fired both his wife and two of his sisters and a niece. And they threatened him with bodily harm. And they sued him on trumped-up charges and convicted him in a kangaroo court.... And they burned his house to the ground while the fire department stood around watching the flames consume the night. And they stoned the church at which he pastored. And fired shotguns at him out of the dark...All of this happened because he was black and brave. And because others followed when he had decided the time had come to lead.

Prior to the *Brown* decision, many whites in positions of influence had also taken significant steps to prepare the intellectual, political and cultural ground for the Court's desegregation ruling. Branch Rickey broke the color barrier in baseball by signing Jackie Robinson in 1945. President Truman ordered the desegregation of the armed forces and the federal civil service in 1948. In the years preceding *Brown,* New Jersey, Indiana and Illinois passed laws prohibiting racial segregation in schooling. Moreover, the Court itself had helped to prepare the legal and political groundwork for *Brown* in successive decisions rendered in the '30s and '40s. The Court cast a pall over the legitimacy of racial distinctions in the law and dramatically increased the cost of segregation. For example, in *Missouri ex rel. Gaines v. Canada* (1938), the Court held that a state could exclude blacks from its white law school only if it took the extremely expensive step of creating within the state a separate but equal law school open to blacks. Later, in *Swett v. Painter* (1950), the Court held that Texas' racially separate law schools were not, in fact, equal and cast doubt on whether, henceforth, it would ever again deem segregated public institutions to be equal. When *Brown* finally came before the Court, the U.S. solicitor general joined with Thurgood Marshall and the National Association of Colored People in calling for the Court to invalidate de jure segregation. After the Court's landmark decision, the *New York Times, Time* and other key organs of public opinion lauded the justices.

The point here is not to disparage what the Court did in *Brown,* a ruling that constitutes a major step upwards in the legal and moral history of the United States. I am simply emphasizing that the decision was the product of justices who had all been certified as members of the power elite and were therefore unlikely to undertake rash projects. By striking down racial segregation in public schooling, the Court did take on a powerful foe—the white supremacist militants of the South. And the struggle set off by *Brown* was protracted. But the decision did not mark a dramatic break from the legal thinking of the time. Nor did the Court go into this battle alone. Nor was it confronting a policy backed by pervasive support throughout the nation. By 1954, open, comprehensive, statutorily required racial segregation in public schools existed only in the South and was viewed as an anachronistic, destructive, embarrassing policy by ever-increasing numbers of Americans. While the justices acted rightly in *Brown,* they did not act as the lonely, heroic crusading figures that often emerge in journalists' accounts of this important decision.

A related problem is journalists' sentimentality about how the justices typically go about their business. In *Gideon's Trumpet,* Lewis wrote that the Court is enabled to lead and enlighten public opinion because justices, armed with life tenure, "are enabled to search for principle, free from the political passions of the moment." According to Lewis, "the independence given to the justices enables them to do things that others know are right but have never had the courage or the determination to do by themselves." Lewis concedes, as he must, that the judgments of justices are shaped by their backgrounds and experiences. But he also maintains that "a Supreme Court justice is more likely than most to outgrow parochial prejudice."

In Lewis' estimation, the Court is far more intellectually exacting and robustly principled than the Congress. In his words, "the diffused, discursive methods of the legislature reflect the fact that its decisions must be political, reflecting compromises and accommodations of interests that may be concerned with issues entirely apart from the one under consideration." By contrast, Lewis maintains, we demand of Supreme Court justices "a process of reason. They must not be legislators, engaged in political bargaining, but lawyers, reasoning by analogy from limited materials, creating the new from the old, shaping experience and ideals into workable principle."

This conception of the Court remains influential; recall that it was confirmed by Linda Greenhouse. And it is partially correct. Clearly the ethos, customs, pace, imperatives and powers of the Supreme Court differ in important ways from those of the Congress and the presidency. But in their anxious efforts to differentiate judges from politicians (and law from politics), journalists of the Lewis and Greenhouse persuasion way overshoot the mark.

When *Brown* and *Gideon* were decided (as in every period before and since), the justices, concerned by or swept up by what Lewis calls "the political passions of the moment," repeatedly rendered decisions that reflected "compromises and accommodations of interests," sometimes over issues "entirely apart from the one under consideration." Chief Justice Earl Warren wrote a purposefully oblique opinion in *Brown v. Board of Education* to avoid angering Southern whites, to cement the Court's own tenuous unanimity and to preserve the Court's own political capital. After *Brown,* the Warren Court refused for over a decade to consider the constitutionality of state statutes prohibiting interracial marriages. The justices were afraid of adverse public reaction if they invalidated such statutes before the public was "ready" for such a step;

they nullified such laws in 1967 only after most states had already rescinded them. As for acting in a fundamentally different fashion from legislators, it is useful to note that the very justice whom Anthony Lewis and many other journalists most admired—William J. Brennan—was famous for his political talents, his ability to wheel and deal to stitch together winning coalitions. Brennan impressed upon his law clerks the importance of remembering and adapting themselves to what he called the Rule of Five—the fact that it takes five votes to win a case. Brennan was correct, of course. But his focus on the Rule of Five, with its blunt, practical attentiveness to the mechanics of power, suggests a decision-making process very different from the cloistered, scholastic, transcendental proceedings that Lewis, Greenhouse and like-minded journalists have popularized.

An alternative is a journalistic tradition that insists upon viewing the justices in the same light as other high-ranking, power-wielding government officials. The proponents of this approach are impatient with customs that shield justices from public exposure. They are also suspicious of the justices' high-sounding (and self-serving) descriptions of themselves. The most important book in this tradition over the past 30 years is *The Brethren* by Bob Woodward and Scott Armstrong, then reporters with the *Washington Post*.

The Brethren stunned Court gazers with detailed revelations about life inside the marble palace of the Court between 1969 and 1976. It reported on gossip, overheard conversations, friendships, rivalries, working habits, quirks, prejudices, justices' methods of communication and negotiation, and the complex ways in which the justices' rulings took shape.

Woodward and Armstrong engage in equal-opportunity muckraking. Unlike Lewis, who sought to advance the liberal tendencies of the Warren Court by praising it and making its ethos the standard against which to measure subsequent Courts, Woodward and Armstrong even-handedly display the unimpressive underbellies of the justices regardless of their leanings. They make Richard Nixon's Chief Justice Warren Burger look bad, but they make Lyndon Johnson's historic appointee, Thurgood Marshall (the first black justice) look bad as well. Woodward and Armstrong appear to have been drawn to their subject not by any substantive agreement or disagreement with the Court's holdings but instead by a particular feature of its decision-making process. The Court's "internal debates...negotiations, confrontations, and compromises," they complain, are "hidden from public view." This is a problem, they write, because "much of recent history, notably the period that included the Vietnam War and the multiple scandals known as Watergate, suggests that the detailed steps of decision making [and] the often hidden motives of the decision makers can be as important as the eventual decisions themselves. Yet the Court," they lament, "unlike the Congress and Presidency, has by and large escaped public scrutiny."

Woodward and Armstrong subjected the Court to unprecedented scrutiny. One of their most effective approaches was to elicit the assistance of the justices' law clerks. They convinced many clerks to share not just their impressions of their bosses, but confidential documents such as internal memoranda and drafts of opinions. Consequently, *The Brethren* sometimes exaggerates the influence of clerks, who, like many sources, are often vain. But the overall result is a detailed, fascinating, instructive and unsparing description of life at the top of the federal judiciary.

The portrait rendered is by no means pretty. But it is at least realistic, confirming a proposition that should never have been in doubt—that the justices are subject to the prevailing prejudices of their era and the ubiquitous vices of humankind. Yes, what the justices read in the newspapers and gather from their conversations with friends and family does affect their rulings. Yes, bruising the ego of a justice can influence the way he or she will vote. (According to Woodward and Armstrong, and there is reason to believe their account, Justice Brennan once decided to vote with the minority in a case simply to deprive Chief Justice Burger of the power to assign him a boring case.) Yes, personal quirks do shape conclusions. (Justice Hugo Black, famous for his expansive interpretation of the First Amendment, voted to uphold the conviction of a man arrested for wearing a jacket in a courthouse that was emblazoned "Fuck the Draft" because the idea of his wife having to view the phrase was too loathsome for him to tolerate.) Yes, most of the justices do act like Cabinet officers, members of Congress and presidents insofar as they delegate to skilled underlings the task of putting their bosses' conclusions into acceptable language. (Woodward and Armstrong reveal that the most famous sentence in the "Fuck the draft" decision of *Cohen v. California*—"One man's vulgarity is another man's lyric"—was penned by a clerk and not the official author of the Court's judgment, Justice John Marshall Harlan.) Yes, justices do join opinions with which they disagree for the purpose of creating bargaining chips.

The Brethren continues to exert an appreciable influence in journalists' circles, strengthening the impulse toward a more probing assessment of the Court's performance, procedures and personnel. This influence can be seen in David G. Savage's *Turning Right: The Making of the Rehnquist Supreme Court,* which is, in many respects, an updated (but pallid) version of *The Brethren,* and in the spate of books that recount the behind-the-scenes struggles at the Senate confirmation hearings of Robert Bork and Clarence Thomas.

Some observers excoriated aggressive coverage of those hearings on the grounds that it was, to paraphrase Greenhouse, cynical, adversarial, partisan and sensationalistic. There is probably some merit to this complaint. But far more problematic than the occasional overreaching or pettiness that some journalists have displayed (one thinks here of the reporters who sought to obtain records of Robert Bork's video rentals), is the very large extent to which, in general, and despite the popular success of *The Brethren,* reporters who cover the Supreme Court continue to adopt a role more befitting of publicists than journalists.

Passive, feel-good coverage of confirmation hearings is especially deplorable given that these are the occasions on which many Americans obtain their only significant impressions of the people who become America's living constitution. Unfortunately, because many journalists are insufficiently probing in their assessment of the confirmation process, large sectors of the public remain unaware that most confirmation hearings are hollow ceremonies where, in exchange for life tenure on the bench, lawyers must mouth fatuous lines that mark them as either ignorant (if they really believe what they say) or duplicitous (if they self-consciously mislead their interrogators). A classic example of this charade arises at that point in confirmation hearings when a senator asks a nominee to state his or her opinion about a controversial Court decision. At her confirmation hearings, when Sandra Day O'Connor was asked about *Roe v. Wade,* which granted a woman a constitutional right to an abortion under certain conditions, she refused to answer most questions put to her. She stated that she could not endorse or criticize specific Supreme Court decisions presenting issues that may well come before the Court again: "To do so would mean I have prejudged the matter or have morally committed myself to a certain position. Such a statement by me as to how I might resolve a particular issue or what I might do in a future Court action might make it necessary to disqualify myself on the matter."

Many leading reporters applaud this sort of evasion and criticize senators for daring to ask questions that prompt it. One doubts, ho ever, whether these same journalists would be so tolerant if a nominee refused to endorse or criticize major decisions such as *Plessy v. Ferguson* (upholding racial segregation in public intrastate transportation) or *Marbury v. Madison* (asserting authority of the Supreme Court to invalidate congressional statutes deemed to violate the federal Constitution), even though important and controversial aspects of these decisions continually reappear on the Court's docket.

Part of reporters' difficulty with acknowledging judicial politics stems from their difficulty with acknowledging journalistic politics. A useful illustration of this point is provided by *Strange Justice: The Selling of Clarence Thomas* by Jane Mayer and Jill Abramson, then, respectively, a senior writer and deputy Washington bureau chief for the *Wall Street Journal*. *Strange Justice,* a critique of Thomas and the campaign to secure his seat on the Court, concludes that at his infamous hearings before the Senate Judiciary Committee, he misled the nation about his views and his interactions with Anita Hill, the subordinate who accused him of sexually harassing her when he chaired the Equal Employment Opportunity Commission. One of the interesting features of the book is that its authors mimic their quarry by engaging constantly in an ideological cover-up.

Nominee Thomas asserted during his confirmation hearings that, as a justice, he would eliminate any personal agendas and ideologies. "When one becomes a judge," he declared, "you begin to decline forming opinions in areas that could come before your court because you want to be stripped down like a boxer." That statement is absurd, both descriptively and prescriptively. It flies in the face of what we know (or should know) about the way that people (especially ambitious people) think and act (and ought to think and act). Can anyone reasonably expect a justice not to feel strongly about freedom of expression, race and gender conflicts, the extent to which society should trust or distrust police officers or the relationship of the federal government to state governments? Far from being reassuring, Justice Thomas' notion of the judicial blank slate is positively frightening. Any jurist who does not have strong, well-formed ideas about the controversies that repeatedly form the backdrop to the Court's cases should be disqualified for a seat on grounds of incompetence. Hence, those who now express disappointment because, in their view, Thomas has failed to fulfill his promises are simply venting foolishness. To have credited such promises in the first place was to indulge in llibility.

One detects an echo of Thomas, however, in the preface to the paperback edition of *Strange Justice* where Mayer and Abramson write (and apparently expect readers to believe) that they "entered [their] subject with open minds." A reasonable person ought to credit that claim if all that Mayer and Abramson mean by "open-minded" is that at the outset of their research their conclusions were not wholly and unalterably set. Usually, though, the term means more. An open-minded decision-maker is one who is equally accessible to competing advocates. Under that definition of the term, a reasonable person would have to be downright naive to believe that Mayer and Abramson would evaluate Thomas "open-mindedly." After all, though they never define their politics, it is clear where they stand ideologically by their choice of enemy and mode of attack. The enemy is the hard right within conservative political circles. Their mode of attack is to criticize the hard right for being outside the "mainstream" of American politics (as if being in the mainstream is itself a sign of virtue).

Given Mayer and Abramson's implicit embrace of a rather conventional form of centrist liberalism, it makes no more sense to think that they can be open-minded in assessing Thomas than to think that Thomas can be open-minded in assessing the constitutional claims of advocates for abortion rights, abolition of the death penalty or the protection of affirmative action. The problem here is not that Mayer and Abramson were wrong in concluding that disingenousness, shallowness and regrettably conservative values and politics triumphed when Clarence Thomas effectively became one-ninth of the living constitution of the United States. The problem is that, respecting conventions that cause journalists to shade their own beliefs, Mayer and Abramson were never fully willing and able to state in a straightforward and convincing manner why they really opposed Thomas' confirmation. Moreover, trapped by conventions that unduly exalt the Court, they minimize the scandal they sought to confront by portraying Thomas' elevation as an aberration.

Judging from these books, how, then, should journalists proceed when they write about the Supreme Court?

First, journalists must take pains to master the procedures and rhetoric the justices use in doing their work. An important virtue of the Anthony Lewis/Linda Greenhouse tradition is that those who work within it provide careful and expert reporting. Some journalists, for example, routinely misrepresent the Court's decision to forego reviewing lower courts' rulings as substantive affirmations of those rulings. Lewis and

Greenhouse seldom make such errors. Their love of the Court, which sometimes makes them overly protective of it, also prompts them to master significant but prosaic facts and intricacies that others overlook.

Second, to return to Linda Greenhouse and the controversy at the *New York Times* over identifying federal judges by the presidents who appointed them—journalists should become more realistic than many are now regarding the extent to which politics affects the Supreme Court and, indeed, all courts. Many newspapers routinely identify politicians by their party affiliation, e.g., "Sen. Orrin Hatch (R-Utah). Such an identification does not insinuate that the named politician is the captive of his party. It is simply a piece of information that is often useful in that it gives readers a clue—a limited but helpful one—about the general political background of the politician in question. The same would be true of identifying justices in the manner to which Greenhouse objected.

Noting the party affiliation of the justice or the appointing president should not be taken as a suggestion that the justices are the subservient agents of their political sponsors. It merely acquaints readers with one piece of information that obviously needs to be supplemented with other information in order to make informed assessments about a justice's performance. It also helpfully reminds the public of a fact that is often neglected or minimized by rhetoric that stresses the independence of the judiciary: Electoral politics matters greatly in shaping the Supreme Court (and the entire federal judiciary) insofar as voter-conscious senators must confirm the choices of voter-conscious presidents. In such a setting, to be inattentive to the political sponsorship of justices or aspiring justices is to be inattentive to the complex realities of the American legal system—a system nourished for the good and bad by the imperatives of electoral power.

Third, journalists should learn a lesson from legal scholars and be open about their own ideological biases. Everyone has them; there is no such thing as the unbiased observer. To recognize and concede one's own ideological proclivities need not prevent a journalist from offering accurate reportage and insightful analysis. Indeed, the reverse is more likely: The reporter who is more self-conscious and open about his or her ideological leanings is likely to be a more sophisticated and credible analyst.

Consider the case of Laurence H. Tribe, a professor at Harvard Law School, the most learned, able and insightful Court watcher in the United States today. His treatise on *Constitutional Law* is a staple at the Supreme Court, and he is cited as an authority even by those who disagree violently with his (liberal) political views. In the introduction to that treatise, Tribe eschews "illusory neutrality," announces his intention to openly avow his substantive beliefs and commitments and does so consistently throughout his massive work. Far from diminishing the intellectual value of his treatise, Tribe's open self-consciousness about his politics adds to its value by making clear the premises that influence his assessments. Tribe's approach should serve as an inspiration to journalists who cover the Court.

Fourth, journalists should incorporate into their work the lessons of social historians who have shown that what emerges into view as large, dramatic events are often the accretion of small, quiet developments that have escaped notice. The great merit of Kluger's *Simple Justice,* for example, is that it redistributes the attention given to the actors in the drama that was *Brown v. Board of Education.* It gives proper credit to the justices' role. But it also gives proper credit to the actions of obscure people in various walks of life whose contributions, long predating 1954, significantly affected the environment in which the ultimate decisions were made. In covering a Supreme Court decision, it may be that the most significant and illuminating story is to be found not in Washington, but in the unheralded places where people stand up to assert their claims.

Fifth, because an informed citizenry is the best protection for a decent democracy, journalists should inform the public *fully* about the Court, even if doing so will likely undermine public respect for the justices. They should not act as the justices' publicists.

Randall Kennedy, a professor at Harvard Law School, is the author of Race, Crime and the Law. *From 1982 to 1983 he was a clerk for Supreme Court Justice Thurgood Marshall.*

For Further Reading

American Bar Association. *The Reporter's Key: Rights of Fair Trial and Free Press.* Chicago: American Bar Association, 1994.

———. *ABA Standards for Criminal Justice: Fair Trial and Free Press.* Washington, D.C.: American Bar Association, 1992.

Atwood, Barbara Ann. *A Courtroom of Her Own: The Life and Work of Mary Anne Richey.* Durham, N.C.: Carolina Academic Press, 1997.

Barber, Susanna. *News Cameras in the Courtroom: A Free Press-Fair Trial Debate.* Norwood, N.J.: Ablex Publishing, 1987.

Bergman, Paul, and Michael Asimow. *Reel Justice: The Courtroom Goes to the Movies.* Kansas City: Andrews and McMeel, 1996.

Brill, Steven. "How the Willie Smith Show Changed America." *American Lawyer,* January-February 1992: 98–102.

Bunker, Matthew D. *Justice and the Media: Reconciling Fair Trials and a Free Press.* Mahwah, N.J.: Lawrence Erlbaum Associates, 1997.

Campbell, Douglas S. *Free Press v. Fair Trial: Supreme Court Decisions Since 1807.* Westport, Conn.: Praeger, 1994.

Carter, T. Barton, Marc A. Franklin and Jay B. Wright. *The First Amendment and the Fourth Estate: The Law of Mass Media.* Westbury, N.Y.: Foundation Press, 1988.

Cuklanz, Lisa M. *Rape on trial: How the Mass Media Construct Legal Reform and Social Change.* Philadelphia: University of Pennsylvania Press, 1996.

Denniston, Lyle W. *The Reporter and the Law: Techniques of Covering the Courts.* New York: Columbia University Press, 1992.

Deutsch, Linda, and Michael Fleeman. *Verdict: The Chronicle of the O.J. Simpson Trial.* Kansas City, Mo.: Andrews and McMeel, 1995.

Felsher, Howard, and Michael Rosen. *The Press in the Jury Box.* New York: MacMillan, 1966.

Freedman, Warren. *Press and Media Access to the Criminal Courtroom.* New York: Quorom Books, 1988.

Gillmor, Donald M., and Jerome A. Barron. *Mass Communication Law: Cases and Comment.* St. Paul, Minn.: West Publishing Company, 1984.

Hariman, Robert, ed. *Popular Trials: Rhetoric, Mass Media, and the Law.* Tuscaloosa: University of Alabama Press, 1990.

Hixson, Richard F. *Mass Media and the Constitution: An Encyclopedia of Supreme Court Decisions.* New York: Garland, 1989.

Holsinger, Ralph L., and Jon Paul Dilts. *Media Law.* New York: McGraw-Hill, 1994.

Kane, Peter E. *Murder, Courts, and the Press: Issues in Free Press/Fair Trial.* Carbondale: Southern Illinois University Press, 1992.

Kluger, Richard. *Simple Justice: The History of Brown v. Board of Education and Black America's Struggle for Equality.* New York: Knopf, 1976.

Kronenwetter, Michael. *Free Press v. Fair Trial: Television and Other Media in the Courtroom.* New York: F. Watts, 1986.

Lewis, Anthony. *Make No Law: The Sullivan Case and the First Amendment.* New York: Random House, 1991.

————. *Gideon's Trumpet.* New York: Random House, 1964.

Mayer, Jane, and Jill Abramson. *Strange Justice: The Selling of Clarence Thomas.* Boston: Houghton Mifflin Co., 1994.

Postman, Neil, and Steve Powers. *How to Watch TV News.* New York: Penguin, 1992.

Reardon, Paul C., and Clifton Daniel. *Fair Trial and Free Press.* Washington: American Enterprise Institute for Public Policy Research, 1968.

Rowan, Carl Thomas. *Dream Makers, Dream Breakers: The World of Justice Thurgood Marshall.* Boston: Little, Brown & Co., 1993.

Rudenstine, David. *The Day the Presses Stopped: A History of the Pentagon Papers Case.* Berkeley: University of California Press, 1996.

Surette, Ray. *Media, Crime, and Criminal Justice: Images and Realities.* Pacific Grove, Calif.: Brooks/Cole, 1992.

Thaler, Paul. *The Spectacle: Media and the Making of the O.J. Simpson Story.* Westport, Conn.: Praeger, 1997.

————. *The Watchful Eye: American Justice in the Age of the Television Trial.* Westport, Conn.: Praeger, 1994.

Toobin, Jeffrey. *The Run of His Life: The People v. O.J. Simpson.* New York: Random House, 1996.

Tucher, Andie. *Froth and Scum: Truth, Beauty, Goodness, and the Ax Murder in America's First Mass Medium.* Chapel Hill: University of North Carolina Press, 1994.

Woodward, Bob, and Scott Armstrong. *The Brethren: Inside the Supreme Court.* New York: Simon and Schuster, 1979.

Law Review Articles

Chemerinsky, Erwin, and Laurie Levenson. "The Ethics of Being a Commentator." *Southern California Law Review* 69 (1996): 1303.

————. "The Ethics of Being a Commentator II." *Santa Clara Law Review* 37 (1997): 913.

Hardaway, Robert, and Douglas B. Tumminello. "Pretrial Publicity in Criminal Cases of National Notoriety: Constructing a Remedy for the Remediless Wrong." *American University Law Review* (October 1996): 39.

Lassiter, Christo. "The Appearance of Justice: TV or Not TV—That Is the Question." *Journal of Criminal Law and Criminology* (Spring 1996): 928.
Whitebread, Charles H., and Darrell W. Contreras. "Free Press v. Fair Trial: Protecting the Criminal Defendant's Rights in a Highly Publicized Trial by Applying the Sheppard-Mu'min Remedy." *Southern California Law Review* 69 (1996): 1587.

Index